WHY I HATED CHRISTIANS

A TRUE STORY

WHY I HATED CHRISTIANS

A TRUE STORY

MICHAEL LOPEZ

ISBN-13
979-8-9876191-0-0 Paperback
979-8-9876191-1-7 eBook
LCCN: 2023904198

The Tough Fight Media
Colorado Springs, CO

Michael recently said to me "You haven't paid for anything, your parents robbed you". So full of wisdom, he is.

For over 17 years I have known Michael and he has always been fair and honest. He has always heard others' reasoning and points of views without hesitation and with understanding. It takes a lot to change his mind though, and he was firm on not believing in God.

When I met Mike, I was a believer, and he was not. Over the years to hear him have discussions with his parents about faith, grace, the good Word, and our Savior, Jesus & how he just wouldn't "go for it". It was always a firm "I just don't know mom" he was very unmoved.

In August of 2021 I started to mourn the relationship and marriage I had built with Mike. I believe he was spoken to that day on the 18th. The changes came fast and with open arms. He and I were changing, and it was difficult, but God grew us together. Mike was spoken to on my Birthday, and what we now consider his Holy Spirit baptism. I can say with my heart, anyone who knew Mike prior to August of 2021 would instantly see the difference God has made in Mike in this year and a half, in our family and professional lives. I know that within reading this book, you'll see the changes the Lord has made in Mike's life, and He only helps Mike to continue to grow in all ways.

-Michaela Lopez

TABLE OF CONTENTS

FOREWORD

I n Mark Chapter 4, Jesus is teaching on the parable of the sower, from a boat, to a crowd of people that had gathered beside the sea on the land. In His teaching. He said to them: Listen! Behold, a sower went out to sow. And as he sowed , some seed fell along the path, and birds came and devoured it. Other seed fell on rocky ground, where it did not have much soil, and immediately it spring up, since it had no depth of soil. And when the sun rose, it was scorched, and since it had no roots, it withered away. Other seed fell among thorns, and the thorns grew up and choked it, and it yield no grain. And other seeds fell into good ground and produced grain, growing up and increasing and yielding thirtyfold and sixtyfold and hundredfold. And He said, "He who has ears to hear, let him hear.

Since you have taken the time to read the first paragraph, it is with great honor and a privilege to write the Forward in this book "Why I Hated Christians" for Mr. Mike Lopez.

Mike and I met in Colorado Springs in 2020 at Villa Sierra Condo Community. He was the owner of the Landscape company that provided landscape services for the Association. I was a Board of Directors with the position as Chairman of the Landscape Committee. Because of my position, I was the watchman over the landscape beautification and services performed by Mike's company.

At the appointment of this position, I had no prior knowledge of Mike or his company. Therefore, as Chair of Landscape, the first thing I did was read his contract to get familiar with the services he was providing. To get a clear understanding of the services and terminology, I scheduled a meeting with Mike to discuss the contract. His first statement to me was, "I have never had any of my clients question me about my contract." He seemed to be a little put out that I was asking him about services in the contract. Well, since I had been a salesman for a Landscape company in Texas, I had knowledge about the landscape business and would often relate to him how things were done in Texas. However, because of his experience as an owner in the business, our opinions would clash at times. One day he looked at me and said, "Let me tell you how we do landscaping in Colorado Springs. There was a sense he was tired of me referring to how landscape business was done in Texas. He was also putting me in my place for challenging his professionalism as the company owner. Upon his explanation, the Holy Spirt instructed me to sow Proverbs 11:3 into him, "The integrity of the upright shall direct their path". This Scripture was a guiding light for me in sales and serving customers for 30 plus years. It's also a Scripture I use in my personal life daily.

Little did I know that Scripture pierced him to the dividing asunder of his soul and spirit (Hebrews 4:12 KJV). Also, I did not know that he "Hated Christians" and here I was sowing the Word at our business meeting which was offense and unethical in his world of doing business, but not so in my kingdom of doing business. What I learned later was he not only felt I was challenging his professionalism but with that Scripture I was challenging his integrity, and I am a Christian, and He Hated Christians!! Some months later after this, he and I were talking about his responsibly as the landscape company and my responsibility to him as the chairman of landscape. I said to him, "I am responsible vertically to God first for all my actions according to His Word. And secondly horizontally it keeps my relationship flowing with courtesy and respect with people I associate with.

Many times, Mike would ask a question about the Bible or God, and the question seemed so unrelated at the time. But as you will read in his book, one of the tactics he enjoyed was tripping Christians up with off the cuff questions because he saw them as weak! Instead of giving him an answer, I would answer his question with a question. He would then have to think about his question.

As the months went by Mike began to ask questions but his questions seem to be coming from a place of "I really want to know, can you help me?" About this time, all of our meeting conversations would transition to the Gospel and in most cases would end on the gospel. In I short time, it was apparent Mike was hungry for the things of God.

I can remember one day I was talking with him and his assistant about the conversations I have with God and hearing the Holy Spirit's voice. He told me later that he and his assistant joked about me hearing voices. It wasn't but a short time after that he had an encounter in his car with the Holy Spirit speaking to him. That divine encounter marked his thinking about Christianity!

In this book he describes me as a tall man with a deep accent and always wearing a cap with Texas on it. He shared later that the more I sowed the Word in our conversations the more it broke his resistance down. He said thank you Maceo for not stopping it has changed my life forever! *Romans 1:16 KJV,*

"For I am not ashamed of the gospel, for it is the power of God to salvation for everyone who believe.

Mike did not write this book for himself, he's sowing his testimony that it may answer a question, give a revelation, or bring someone into the reality of the Christian life. John 14:6 NIV, Jesus answered, "I am the way and the truth and the life. No one comes to the Father except through me." Proverbs 9:9, Give instruction to a wise man and he will be yet wiser; teach a righteous man (one upright and in right standing with God) and he will increase in learning.

Mike invited my wife and I to his home for dinner and we met his family. At dinner his wife said, "Maceo, Mike has made a 180 degree change since he met you, and his change has affected me to change as well".

I am Dr. Maceo Smith: Teacher, Author, Minister, Mike's Encourager, and Founder of Encourage U-On Ministry. In my book "What Is Meditating God's Word...Become Wiser and Increase Your Learning" there is this statement... When you read Scripture read it in the first person, make it personal by putting your name in the Scripture because it's God speaking to you. Mike recently had an opportunity to sow a brief part of his testimony at his Church and he made reference to him reading my book and began putting his name in Scripture and how the reality of ownership began to manifest in his life from the Scripture.

My wife Brenda and I congratulate Mike and his entire family for this inspiring testimony in the pages of this book, "Why I Hated Christians". We also consider it a privilege and honor to call him FRIEND!

Proverbs 3:27 NKJV, "Do not withhold good from those whom it is due, When it is in the power of your hand to do so."

Dr. Maceo Smith
Encourage U-On Ministry
Teaching Spiritual Growth through Biblical Meditation
Pottsboro, TX.

INTRODUCTION

Lots of People in this world have grown to hate Christians. I was one of them. I have seen firsthand why Christians are written off as arrogant, rude hypocrites! Through this book, I hope to create an understanding between Christians and those that dislike them with the knowledge I have gained by being both an observer and participant.

A big reason many people have grown to hate Christians is because those who claim to be strictly devout to The Bible tend to abuse scripture with how they treat both believers and non-believers alike, as if they are beneath them. Very much unlike the "Christ-like" way, these Christians present themselves as. Therefore, it is crucial to understand the semantics and words used in The Bible when you read it. If you don't, you will not understand the full meaning of what the Scripture intends, and the abuse of the said scripture will continue along with spreading a disdain of Christianity.

This is because words are extremely powerful and hold weight to them when they are used in daily conversation. Generally speaking, the words that come out of your mouth come from a place you may not really be aware exists. In fact, they come from your heart, or your spirit. When you say a word, it is typically generated from a thought right? That thought is generated by what is in your heart (spirit). When we talk and use our words, many people do not always realize what they are really saying.

In this generation and the few preceding it, people have changed definitions. Slang has become the ruling form of communication for many; it is in this context that we can see how some words have lost their meaning. There are some words we have even seen change in official definitions. That should scare anyone who is paying attention. The reason why words are so important and are not to be overlooked is because when we communicate, especially instruction, the definitions make it clear about what we are saying. Think about it, if you tell someone what you want done and you are specific about that need and the said person does it totally opposite of what you instructed, what do you do? How do you feel about that?

Granted we all make mistakes; let's just say that they didn't listen to your instruction; let's say that you told them repeatedly and they simply did not listen. Now how do you feel? Let's go further and say that this instruction that you gave this person was a possible matter of life and death, and they just didn't listen. They failed on their own, no? What if this person told you that the words you used have a different meaning to them? Now it gets complicated.

Remember, you were specific, you explained in detail how this person should perform this task which was a possible matter of life and death, and they debated the definitions of the words that you gave them in that instruction. So, if we are to make our own definitions for words then how are we supposed to effectively communicate anything, important or not?

The words we use and the way that we say things are critical to our way of life and our future; everything we do revolves around communication and understanding. The more we mutilate how we communicate, the further we will get from the concept of understanding. If you are the type of person who believes that words and their true meanings are not important, please try to read this book with the mindset that they do matter, so that you may understand fully what this book is about. Just like fully understanding the scripture in The Bible to grasp its intended message.

So, what is this book about? For the most part it is a narrative description about my battle with Christianity, or Christians if you will. I have written this book in a manner that may not appeal to all, but I am hoping that it can be understood that I am a normal guy with no college education. I wanted to write this book in a fashion that may give the reader the feeling that we are having a conversation in a room together. I admit this book is being written with the mindset of it being an audio book but, as you read on, just remember words and how important their intended meanings are.

CHAPTER 1

MY EARLY EXPERIENCE WITH CHURCHES

Growing up around the Catholic Church and other similar denominations, I became somewhat fond of the "ceremonial" aspect of it all. I always thought the guys with the flags, banners, and the robes were kind of cool. I also liked how "majestic" and "official" it was. To this day, I still have an appreciation for it all. My parents would take us to church on Christmas Eve; it was always so beautiful. My main take away from going to Catholic Church was the exercise. Oh my! The exercise! Sit-stand-kneel, sit-stand-kneel, and on and on it went. I can remember having the worst time paying attention. My mom, the enforcer, would never hesitate to twist my ear to get me in line to "sit up and pay attention".

Of course, I didn't. Well, pay attention anyway. I can always remember the smell of incense as the clergy walked down the aisles. I can remember watching each one of them singing along with the choir. The traditionalism in it is what I appreciate. Oddly enough, I never related any of it to God himself, let alone any teachings of the Bible. It was always just a dreary boring blur. Oh and let's not forget the offering plate. It always seemed so impersonal. Even though I found the Christmas mass to be beautiful, I never particularly found the other masses entertaining in the least bit. In fact, I some-what detested entering churches because I knew I would be made to sit still and be bored out of my mind when all I really wanted to do was go out and play.

When I was a ten-year-old or so, my older sister Elizabeth and I went to visit our grandparents in Loveland, Colorado. My grandparents were very kindhearted, dedicated Christians and were my mother's parents. They would volunteer at their church and it seemed they were a very big part of it. Their church was a big one, or so it seemed at the time, where light would shine in. I would describe it as evangelical. In other words, it wasn't the Gothic style church I was used to. When I went into this church, I remember thinking how weird it looked and how cool it was that it had long hallways. Oh yes, I ran like a track star through them.

My father never really cared for my grandparents. In fact, he never really had much nice to say about them. While he never encouraged me directly to not like my grandparents, hearing him talk bad about them certainly influenced me to not care for them much myself. Plus, let's face it, at that time, around 1986 or so, there were far more important things to worry about than your nerdy, Christian grandparents, right? I mean come on, there were Transformers, G.I. Joe, and Thundercats.

Staying with my grandparents was brutal to say the least. I had no toys to play with at all. My sister and I tried to play out-side but there really wasn't much to do. I begged for toys and my grandma came outside with us and gave me and my sister a plastic box you could grow plants in, a greenhouse if you will. In the box was a few packages of seeds. I can remember vividly thinking, *what the eff am I supposed to do with this?* Thinking back, my lack of respect was likely intolerable.

As I sifted through the house trying to find something that would pique my interest, I stumbled across a small figurine style easel with a ceramic prayer book on it. It was probably about 4" tall. I remember the easel was a dark to medium shade of brown and the book on it was off-white and had pink flowers on it with some writing. The easel…was a SCORE! I took the book off of it and used the easel as an "X-wing" fighter. Finally, I was having some fun! At some point my grandma caught me playing with it. She told me it was not a toy and I had disrespected her home. She brought me over to the end table where it had resided and was upset, I just threw the book onto the table without knowing what I was doing. She told me it was a prayer.

She made me read the prayer as if I was supposed to feel guilty about using the easel as a toy, but I can tell you it had zero impact on me except for making me more irritated that I had nothing to play with. I remember the rest of that trip being nothing short of brutally boring. When we went to their church, I can remember all of the old people coming up to us and saying how cute we were and how we must remember to say our prayers, followed by kisses on our cheeks. UGH! The feeling of being crowded was overwhelming to say the least. The main thing I remember about my grandparents was how incredibly boring they were and how obsessed they seemed with church and God.

Ultimately, this was a contributor to my negative view of Christians, church, and God. As my childhood went on, I did not necessarily dismiss or hate God. There was nothing in my life that made me want to be close to or far from God. I simply did not care.

CHAPTER 2

MY FIRST JOB

I was born in 1976; the Bicentennial in Denver, Colorado. When I was around five years old, our family moved to New Jersey in the Essex County area to the town of Millburn. It was a nice suburban town where many of the men commuted to NYC on the NJ Transit commuter train. I went to first, second, and third grade in Millburn. At the end of the third grade, we moved to the next town over which was called Maplewood, NJ where I spent my fourth through ninth grade years.

Maplewood was a small town as well where most of the men again, commuted to NYC on the train, including my dad. Across the street from my home in Maplewood was a Catholic School called St. Joseph's. They pretty much owned the block with a church, a school, a library, a rectory, a family life center, and a couple of other small houses; which may or may not have belonged to the church. I spent most of my time playing over there as it was somewhat laid out like a maze, or an 80s kid's paradise if you will. Lots of steps to jump your bike off of, play hide and seek, stuff like that.

There was an old man who worked there named George. He was a German man with a German last name which escapes me now. He would chase my friends and I out of there constantly ruining any fun we were having. That's why we would always refer to him as "The Nazi". We were definitely goofballs back then for that. As we got older, George seemed to run out of steam to chase us. One day, I was in the parking lot practicing lacrosse on a bRob wall of the school. It was nice because behind me was a fence so if I missed the ball, it would usually hit the fence. Wouldn't you know on this day, I broke a window on the third floor. As I stood there thinking about what to do, George stuck his head out the window. He said, "Stay there, don't move!" So, I stood there waiting for him to come down and beat me to a pulp or even worse, call the police. He came out and asked me what I was doing and how many times had he told me, my brother, and my friends not to play there. I apologized and told him I would pay for the window. He shook his head and told me he knew a way I could pay it off.

That was when he offered me a job. He said I could pay the window off and then continue to work after school cleaning the Catholic School. Truthfully, it did not sound like a great opportunity. I was a typical lazy kid who just wanted to play outside and set things on fire. The thought of working did not appeal to me.

In 1989, when I was thirteen years old, I was offered about $3.35 an hour, cash if I remember right. I would work there after school every day. I would never, ever forget my Walkman and *always* made sure I had good batteries. I was mostly alone and spent a little bit of time here and there looking at statues and depictions of Jesus, Mary, etc. in the chapel. A couple of years earlier I had gone to the church service at St. Joes with my family to see my neighbor, Pat, off to be buried.

My family was not incredibly religious. We went to church some Sundays but mostly on holidays like Christmas and Easter. I was baptized as a baby in a Roman Catholic church along with the rest of my siblings and my mother was always obsessed to some degree with her Bible. I can remember seeing her sitting in her rocking chair in the attic reading her Bible and almost always crying. I never understood why at the time. To this day, I still see my mother cry when she reads her Bible, at church, or even talking about Jesus.

Anyway, I could remember watching Pat's coffin being rolled down the aisle and seeing everyone in tears. Pat was a Jolly old Irishman who was always kind to us kids. Molly, his wife, was also very kind. She would sit and listen to me while I complained about how awful my parents and my life were. But Pat, Pat was always so jolly and full of smiles and laughter.

Back then, my parents could be quite stern and held me accountable for just about everything, even some things I didn't do. As a typical kid, I contested them of course. Geri, Pat and Molly's daughter, was in her late 20's at the time and had the pleasure of being witness to the crazy antics at "The Lopez House". It was sad to see Pat go. From then on, I associated church with death, along with hospitals in my later days. When you walk into a church seeing death and depression, it can be hard to want to learn more about God.

As I worked at the church/school, I got to know George "The Nazi", very well. He would talk to me about school and my friends. He never missed an opportunity to tell me I needed new ones. As George and I grew slightly closer, I got to be very good at my job as he would always critique me in very non-forgiving ways. When I would complain to my parents, they would always try to solidify how important it was to do my job the best I could, not talk back, and be gracious. I am sure it isn't hard to imagine that in my early teens, it was a tough pill to swallow. I really hated that job.

Yes, George had become a very positive influence in my life and holding me accountable definitely made him that much more of a Nazi in my eyes. See how we throw words around without even thinking about it? However, truth be told, I loved the guy. He drove a late 70's Chevy truck if I remember right, ugly 70's tan. It had a topper on it, and he would always be in to get things out or put things in. He worked very hard and always seemed focused on his job which was strange because, at the time, *I thought I did everything!*

After working at St. Joes for about a year, George left. I did not know he was leaving. He surely did not tell me, nor anyone else for that matter. I found out in the Spring of 1989 when the head priest guy told me as I was signing in. The new boss was a man named Gill. He looked to be a Hispanic man, probably in his late 40's, early 50's. We shook hands and he kind of gave me the look like "this is the kid I have to work with?"

So, it was back to business as usual. After about a week or two of working under Gill, I found he was constantly on me for things that didn't really seem to exist, or that didn't seem important. He would say I missed a spot when I didn't or forgot a trash can because he would find a single Kleenex in it (maybe he put it in there?). Regardless, he made my life pretty tough for about a week. Then the day came when I actually made a mistake, a big one. I took some trash out from the third floor. I didn't know that there was milk in the trash bag, let alone that there was a big hole in it. So, I left a trail of milk splatter through the whole building all the way to the trash area outside.

When I turned around from dropping off the bags, I saw the milk trail. I threw up my hands and yelled out a profanity. All I could think of was how I should have taken the trash out first because that's what I was taught to do. Hmm, George was right after all! As I went back into the building to grab the mop, Gill met me at the door with a not so happy look on his face.

"What in the hell did you do here"?

"There was a hole in the bag," I replied just about ready to clean it up.

"How could you be so stupid to not take the trash out first?" He asked in an irritated tone.

When I apologized and told him I was about to clean the mess up he just snapped and fired me. I was crushed! I LOVED THAT JOB!

CHAPTER 3

MY SECOND JOB AND MY ENTREPRENEURSHIP

Although my first job had nothing to do with Christianity, religion, or any other spiritual being, it did take place in the place of God so a small stain on Christians was made, and it didn't help that a few days later Gil's son was now working there (my first experience in dealing with nepotism).

At that time, my mom worked two or three jobs to try to match my dad's income. My mom did waitressing, worked for a janitorial service as an office assistant, and worked for a shoe store. Through all of that though, she always found time to help the church. My parents seemed to gravitate to a church in Millburn (the next town over where we used to live) called St. Stephen's Episcopal. My mom frequently volunteered at the church and helped out in ministry.

The summer of 1991, my mom came and told me that the church cemetery was looking for some help maintaining the grounds. I agreed because, for some reason, I enjoyed mowing the lawn. Previously, I mowed a few yards on the block and made a couple bucks here and there. Around this time, I also provided a little service to some businesses on Springfield Avenue, a local business artery, where I would go get people lunch, a soda, etc. I would get a buck here and there. I quickly learned to score. On Junk Day once, I found a couple of boxes of small metal lock boxes outside of a bank on my walk home from school. Safety deposit boxes perhaps? My brother and I took them home; they all still had keys. So, we spray painted them and sold them at school. I made some good money on that deal!

The job offer at the cemetery was unbeatable though. Eight dollars an hour under the table! I am not sure why the pay was so high but, needless to say, I took it. Unfortunately, at that same time, the company my dad worked for in NYC was closing its doors. With no real opportunities for him, he decided to move us back to Colorado. So, at the beginning of my last summer in Maplewood, my dad also worked at the cemetery. He worked in the early mornings and I came in around 9am and would work until about 3pm.

The cemetery itself was absolutely beautiful. It was hilly with huge trees and some very old stones. Every day I would mow past the stones and got really familiar with them. There was one stone in particular, Dewitt and Anne Brevoort. Dewitt died 1855 and Anne died 1853. There was a huge tree, Oak I believe, growing around the stone with two vines or top roots that grew out from it. It was almost as if their souls were responsible. From this sight, I developed a love for the dead from a sentimental point of view.

While I maintained the cemetery, I had the pleasure of working with an old man named Mike Socia. He rode around on the John Deere tractor while I had to run the push mower. He would always give me $20 and tell me to run down to the deli to get him a pastrami sandwich on rye and, since I could keep the change, I almost always got a large pizza and a Coke at Lastrada with it. During our lunch break, he would always tell me stories of him growing up and things about his life; he was an interesting man.

During that time, I didn't think much about God. I did wonder quite a bit about death, how people died, where they went, etc. Although it didn't consume me, the time I spent mowing the lawn at that cemetery left a huge mark on my life. Every other Saturday, I had to go into Millburn and mow the church which was about a half mile away from the cemetery. On this particular Saturday, I was not feeling up to mowing. For some reason, I didn't enjoy it. Perhaps it was because the grass areas were exposed to the public. You see, the cemetery was fenced in and surrounded by huge trees so it was "sealed off" from the world.

While mowing around the grass in circles working my way to the center, I had to push the mower under a large bush. While doing so, a hornet the size of a bat crawled **inside** my ear and stung me. I was in excruciating pain. I left the mower there, got on my bike and headed home. Now the distance from the church to my house was about ten minutes in the car and about thirty minutes or so by bike. On my way home I stopped at Quick Check, a local convenience store. I went in and grabbed myself a grape soda and a Hostess Teenage Mutant Ninja Turtle Pie.

When I got home, I sat down and kicked on MTV and started watching videos (this was when MTV actually played videos) and began to eat my pie and drink my grape soda. Soon after, my parents walked in the door. The first thing my dad said was, "What are you doing home? You're supposed to be mowing the church!"

"Dad, I got stung in the ear by a hornet," I said while my face was swollen and my ear was throbbing.

My mom bent down toward me on the couch and yelled, "Oh but you had time to stop and get yourself a snack, didn't you?" What could I possibly say? It got worse. She then continued, "Get on your bike and get back down there and finish your job!"

So that was exactly what I did. That did two things to me. One, I grew a very dedicated work ethic and two, made me really hate churches. Of course, it wasn't the buildings' fault or the people in it, I simply associated the church with misery. I am sure that many do, like the poor souls who had the misfortune and tragedy of being abused in one, or by a member of one who claimed to be righteous. As I attended churches at other places and times, I didn't exactly relate the hornet experience directly but subconsciously, I just did not want to be near churches.

CHAPTER 4

The Kid That Used to Be Me

In my elementary years, I had always wanted to be a jock or in the "cool crowd". Even with these aspirations, I was actually a gigantic nerd. In fact, my first fight, in the fourth grade was with the biggest nerd in school. He put me in a head lock and I couldn't get out. So I yelled that the principal was coming and he let me go. Looking back, I guess I was the biggest nerd in school since I was bullied frequently and got put into a head-lock by the biggest nerd in school.

In the fifth grade, I was hanging out with my little brother. He was a big goofball. He wore nerdy glasses with a strap around them so he wouldn't lose them. He always did though. Once or twice, my sister found them on the sidewalk while walking home from school. When we were kids, my sisters and I always said he was adopted because we all had brown hair and brown eyes while he had blonde hair and blue eyes. I would always pick on my brother because he was so easy to pick on. Plus, I got picked on all the time, so I guess I just was doing what I thought I was supposed to do as a big brother.

Let's not forget, my brother was the baby of the family and always treated better than the rest of us. Oh yes, he was my father's pride and joy and to this day still seems like it sometimes. Don't get me wrong, I harbor no ill feelings toward my dad or my brother for this. Growing up with it, however, was tricky sometimes. I would frequently use my brother to get my way because that was the only way I felt I could do so. For a glimpse into that, let's talk Halloween. Not the holiday necessarily, the movie. Yep, it was Halloween time and Halloween movies were playing on TV. Halloween the movie was on that night while my brother and I were out playing hard in the neighborhood. My mom had been calling us for some time, although, we did not hear her because we went further from the house than we were allowed to. So, when we finally got home, we were in big trouble. My parents sent us to our room and we were not allowed to watch Halloween. I was devastated.

My brother and I shared a room where we had bunk beds. I had the top bunk. Since I knew how much my dad loved my brother, I hung my head down like Long Duck Dong and said to my brother, "Start crying, dad will feel sorry for you and let us come downstairs." He argued with me a little, but it only took a solid threat to get him to change his mind. So, my brother started fake crying.

I kept telling him, "Louder, louder." At least five times my parents yelled at him to shut up and go to sleep. I will be honest here, my plan was for them to feel bad for him so they would let him come downstairs and out of sympathy, let me come down as well.

The plan completely backfired...on my brother. Yes, my plan backfired on him, not me. Finally, after about twenty minutes of wailing, my dad yelled, "Michael, since you aren't crying you can come downstairs and watch Halloween!" Of course, I jumped right out of bed and took off, leaving my brother who then started crying for real. I didn't feel bad about that until later in life. If my memory serves me right, I believe they eventually let him watch the movie as well.

Oddly enough, I was never really jealous of my brother and what seemed to be his special treatment, I just always figured that was how it was. I didn't think a whole lot of myself, so it was never really worth complaining about, I guess. I admit that as an adult, there have been a few times where I was a little resentful but thankfully, I was always strong enough to not harbor or release it onto my brother or my dad.

During the summer of 1987 in the afternoon around 3pm, we were leaving a small convenient store called Russ & Midges. As we walked out, I saw a school bully named James. He was on a really cool bike, a Mongoose. At that time, I really wanted a GT Dyno; or even a GT Performer. The Mongoose was cool and all but the GT, that was the bike to have. For some reason, I yelled at him "That's a gay bike!" (there we go throwing those words round again)

From that, he turned the bike around. He came up to me wearing stone washed jeans with holes in them, had a mullet, pinched face, a spiked necklace, bulging muscles, and seemed like he was ten feet tall. You know the guy. He told me and my brother to sit on the bench outside the store. When I sat down, he asked me what I said, I repeated it and said I was sorry. He grabbed my shirt and raised his fist at me threatening to punch me in the mouth.

Luckily, he didn't. He told me, "Get the hell out of here!"

So, I did just that. Only, when my brother got off the bench, he said, "Not you. Sit down."

I ran home as fast as I could and called my mom and told her that someone was beating up my little brother. At about the same time that my mom was pulling up to the house, my brother was walking up the porch steps. I was so happy to see him. I asked him what happened, and he said, "Nothing."

James just made him sit there for ten minutes or so. At that moment, I was the biggest coward in the world. I vowed that day, to never let anyone in my family be harmed, ever.

Fortunately for me, I ended up making some friends in middle school that taught me to stand up for myself. After beating up one of my bullies in the sixth grade, my life began to change. Come eighth grade, I somehow got the courage to try out for the lacrosse team and I made it! Third string of course. At the end of the season, I had proven to be not such a good player. The team picked on me all the time. "Why are you playing lacrosse Lopez? Do you think you're going to be popular? Do you think you're going to get a girlfriend? Do you think you're going to get any real friends that actually like you?"

I thought all of those things. That was a lot of my motivation. During the last game I played, the coach, for some bizarre reason, put me in the game in the last quarter. The score was really close and I played attack. That means, I would have had an opportunity to win the game. So as the game went on, I ran around trying to make it look like I knew what I was doing. At one point, I was wide open. I yelled to my teammate, "Pass it to me!" To my horror, he did. Luckily enough, I caught the ball. I was about twenty or thirty feet from the goal. I cranked it up and shot it. Unfortunately, the ball went about ten feet above the goal and the goalie didn't even try to reach for it.

Just then, I hear the coach yell, "Lopez, OUT!"

As I was running back to the sideline, one of my teammates that always had something belittling to say was running out to replace me had grabbed me by my face mask and said "You just blew your chance to be popular." I was humiliated! I knew in that moment that I looked like a complete loser and wasn't cut out for sports.

That following summer, I had the honor of attending West Point Lacrosse camp. It was for a week. At camp, no one knew who I was or that I wasn't good at sports. So, you could say, I had a little bit more confidence. I was treated by the other attendees as just another fellow player. The coaches made all of us play every position. I had the misfortune of having to play midfield. I received the ball from a defenseman and made a pretty nice run down field juking three or four players. I could hear the coach yelling, "Pass it!" and when I saw the goalie and remembered what my teammate said to me about blowing my chance to be popular, I got right up to the goal, cocked back, and fired. It went right into the goalie's pocket.

I was crushed. Shortly after the play, the scrimmage ended and we all huddled up. The coach asked everyone, "What did Lopez do wrong?"

Everyone replied, "He didn't pass the ball." I couldn't' understand why I was wrong; I was trying to score man!

The coach then explained, "Always pass it, you're on a team." That was when I realized that I didn't come from a team, I came from a group that hated me. Nevertheless, I was determined now to be great at sports.

That following winter, I joined the wrestling team. Interestingly enough, I wasn't picked on much or at all really. I wasn't that great in the beginning; however, I won my fourth match and felt a need to win after that. I ended up doing OK in wrestling and actually really liked it. In the spring I joined the lacrosse team again. Between camp and playing against the wall at St. Joes almost every day, I felt ready to get in there and be a winner. Though it took all season, I finally was getting some exposure. I was involved in plays and understood them. I was assisting with goals and I was winning.

The great part was my teammates weren't making fun of me anymore. They didn't really talk to me either, but it didn't matter. I could see that I was moving up. That summer, before we left New Jersey, I was invited to a party. I imagined it would be like an 80's movie where the nerd gets invited to the party but ends up getting humiliated or beat up instead. However, I was wrong. I actually had a great time. Even though I didn't stay more than a couple of hours, some of the guys talked to me, some ignored me, but no one picked on me. Finally, I was moving up!

After that summer, my dad did not find a job and he moved us to Colorado. I never wanted to go as I was starting to win in life and felt like I was actually going somewhere. Once I got to Colorado, I became angry. I hung out with the wrong crowd and began to get into all kinds of trouble. I started shop-lifting and soon rapidly got into a much deeper life of crime. I had two sets of friends. One, a group of thugs that lived in my area. Two, a group of thugs that lived on the bad side of town. I would get into fights a lot. We would rob people, mostly drug dealers, and I sold drugs, broke into cars, jumped people, all kinds of bad things.

I actually really enjoyed it and felt that it was what I was supposed to be doing with my life. The days of sports and trying to be someone of value were over and I was now living a completely different life. My almost non-existent relationship with my parents deteriorated into a fairly hateful and turbulent one. Before this, they were just the two people who told me what to do and embarrassed me along the way. I spent most of my time insulting them or even nearly getting physical with them. I felt the need to be in control of these people and I definitely struck fear into my parents on a few occasions. Peter Ustinov said, "Parents are the bones upon which children sharpen their teeth" – Sorry Mom, sorry Dad.

CHAPTER 5

My Battle with Christianity

Community Service at Radiant Church

When I was about sixteen, I was arrested for shop lifting. It was shortly after moving to Colorado. I went to court in the spring of 1992, and the judge gave me eighty hours of community service along with a fine. My community service was to be done at a church called Radiant Church in Colorado Springs on the east end of town. I knew of the church because it wasn't far from home and I had ridden my bike through their parking lot many times.

When I showed up to work, I met a guy who showed me around and taught me how to use the self-propelled vacuum cleaner. SCORE! What an easy job. All I had to do was walk around through the halls and the chapel with this self-propelled vacuum cleaner. I spent two to four hours every time I went. Luckily, it was summer break.

One thing that stood out in my mind was that out of all the places I could have done community service, all were at churches. Why was that? As I got older, I realized that churches like to get whatever they can for free, even child labor. Was it possible that maybe the courts thought it would be a good idea because maybe the young troublemakers would find God while cleaning the bathrooms and vacuuming the floors? I never saw that. In fact, not once did any of the church staff ever bring up the subject.

On an ironic note, while I was looking through one of the refrigerators one day, I saw a pack of hot dogs and stole them.

Youth Group – Rob and Marissa

Oddly enough, one of the groups of thugs I hung out with in my area went to a church youth group. What a hypocrisy right? So, at some point, they talked me into going with them, even though I really didn't want to go. My biggest motivator to go was a girl named Marissa whom I had a crush on. So of course I went. I got to be a little bit closer to her. Although she was nice to me, I didn't seem to be her type.

Throughout my time at the youth group, I would say about a year, our pastor was a young 24year-old man by the name of Rob. I was sixteen or seventeen at the time and most of the friends that I attended with were about the same age. At some point in the youth group, there was a group prayer. We'd stand in a circle holding hands while someone would pray out loud, so it looked like we were all praying together. I began to feel a deep sense of fear in that circle. I am not sure what it was that I was feeling but I can say that it impacted me mentally and physically. Was it my emotions going crazy because I knew that everything I was doing in life was wrong? Could it have been The Holy Spirit? Unfortunately, I wasn't paying close enough attention to my inner self to know.

Rob was a great pastor. He made a lot of sense in what he was preaching even though I still didn't buy most of it because I simply didn't see the point, I didn't see a benefit, I didn't see *me* in any of it. However, one of his sermons stuck with me even till now.

"You see, as Christians, we can't live our lives in sin just because Jesus will forgive us. We have to live righteously and repent when we do sin so that we will be accepted into heaven. If you live your life in sin expecting forgiveness, then it won't count, and you will be a hypocrite. You can't walk through life, believing in God but not committing to God. When the trumpets sound on the day of the rapture, you can't stop and turn around and say "I love Jesus!" and be saved! No! You are saved NOW, and you live the rest of your life like you have been saved!"

Those words were powerful to me. It really made me understand from an outside perspective what the commitment to God was all about and how extensive it really was. I really didn't understand the Bible, let alone take any interest in reading it. A few years before we moved to Colorado, my grandparents had bought me one for my birthday or Christmas, but I had thrown it into a box and forgotten about it. I brought it to youth group once but felt really weird carrying it, let alone reading it. I opened the Bible to a random page and read a passage. It spoke to me directly about something that was going on in my life at the time. Strange looking back that in about five or six different moments in my life, I had that same experience. If I knew then what I know now, I would have written it down.

I think it was in early spring when we were in youth group listening to Rob. Toward the end of the service, he had a special announcement to make. Rob was leaving us. Apparently, he was leaving town with his girlfriend to another place. As he spouted off his departure speech, Marissa began to cry almost uncontrollably. There had been rumors going around that Marissa was in love with Rob. No one, however, could predict what was to come. As Rob said his final words, Marissa jumped out of her seat and ran to Rob and wrapped her arms around him. As she was wrapped around him in tears, the rest of the group got up and did the same. Except for me. I just sat there for a minute. I had a feeling something was very wrong. Perhaps I was jealous that Rob got more attention than

I did from Marissa. Perhaps the rumors were true, and I was upset about it. No, maybe both. Bottom line, I knew something wasn't right. Finally, I got up and went over and hugged the crowd as everyone else did. That was the last time I attended youth group.

Not long after that, it turned out that Rob was wanted by the law for statutory rape. Oh yes, Rob and fifteen-year-old Marissa were an item behind closed doors. I was crushed and repulsed all at the same time. In the following days of the news, I thought about that an awful lot. Not just the Marissa portion but, what I learned about God, Jesus, and Christianity. This guy that I looked up to, that was supposed to be our teacher and spiritual guide, the one who taught us about the evil of hypocrisy, not only broke the law for lust but cheated on his girlfriend or fiancé.

A positive Christian role model in my life had instantly been reduced to rubble and along with him, God.

G.W. and His Church - Baptism

Around this time, I had a friend who went by the name of G.W. He was a black kid my age and we shared a passionate interest in comic books. G.W. was different from the rest of my friends. He was good, honest, and caring soul. He was a devout Christian even at our age which I thought was weird and frankly, lame. G.W. and I began to compose a story and invent a few characters to create our own comic book. Throughout our friendship, I would tell him things that I did with my friends like steal car stereos or get into fights. He would always tell me how I needed Jesus.

I didn't agree of course. I didn't slam G.W. or try to mock him in any way. I did tell him about Rob though. He told me that hypocrites are going to come and go but that it is up to us to stay straight and narrow. The mark that Rob's let down left on me was dark. So, to listen to G.W. talk about God and

Jesus was a waste of time for me. We got to be close friends, but I never hung out with him and my criminal friends at the same time. When he would see us in the hallways at school, we would always acknowledge each other but he would never hang out. He'd always respectfully declined.

I never gave him a hard time for this, but I can honestly say that I found him to come off as being better than everybody else. Somewhat arrogant even. Still, he was a goodhearted person to say the least. Eventually, G.W. became a bit vocal about how I was living my life. Not insulting, but vocal. He would tell me how my friends weren't really my friends because they were allowing me to do wrong deeds with them. It started to make sense to me on a small level. Of course, I understood him very well but as a young and dumb fool, I resisted so that I could indulge in my temptations.

At some point, G.W. finally influenced me to go to his church. When I went, the people there were very kind to me. I was influenced by them and G.W. to get baptized. I had only gone to this church a few times. I'm not really sure why I agreed to do it, but I guess I wanted to appease the people and a small part of me wanted to make a change in my life as I was constantly getting into trouble with the law. I remember putting on some sort of tarp. I stepped down into the pool and was baptized. I had no real clue of what I was doing. Even though the church people explained it in great detail, I wasn't developed enough to fully comprehend the event. That was the last time I attended G.W.'s church. After that in fact, I stopped hanging out with him altogether or maybe he stopped hanging out with me.

I felt like G.W. was pushy. Almost like he kind of forced me into it. I wasn't mad at him and I didn't think any less of him, I just felt pressured. It really wasn't my thing but for some reason I did it anyway.

My Mom and Her Secret Life

My mother was a devout Christian and would try to be consistent in having me say my prayers in my younger days. Although she wasn't very outspoken about her faith to any of us, I did see that she devoted much of her time to the church and other noble causes. So, at heart, my mom was a great person.

Growing up, I was frequently angry. One big reason was because my parents fought constantly. They didn't really get along much. I don't remember many times where my parents seemed like two people that loved each other. Their relationship seemed almost contractual more than mutual. My mom was always the enforcer while my dad was more of the funny one. Can you believe that dad?

Over the years, many things happened during that time that I did not understand. In about 1987 or so, I can remember a hot summer day where my parents were yelling and screaming at each other. Me, my sisters, and my brother were playing upstairs. After what seemed like days of fighting, my dad called my older sister and I to the top of the stairs. They started asking us who we wanted to live with. I don't remember what my sister said but I started crying. Even though I couldn't stand my parents, I didn't want them to split up. Thankfully that didn't happen.

Within a year or two afterwards, a man called our house and asked for my mom. My little sister answered the phone and when he asked for my mom, she cussed him out and told him not to call again. I'm not sure to this day why her reaction was like that, but she got her mouth washed out with soap for it, which at the time, I thought was hysterical.

Sometime after that, my dad took her and my brother in the car and drove by my mom's work. All I can remember is that it had something to do with suspicion and that it left some kind of mark in my brother and sister's minds.

1994 was of the worst years of my life. I was supposed to graduate high school that year. Since we had picked up and moved to Colorado from New Jersey right after I had my first year of high school, I was one angry S.O.B. because I WAS FINALLY WINNING! I was creating a decent life for myself, doing decent in sports, school and socially. I felt like I was in one of those 80's movies where the nerd becomes popular. Even though I wasn't at that peak yet, I was on my way. After having that ripped away from me, I became unforgiving toward anything involving anyone.

I was fighting constantly, stealing anything that wasn't nailed down, destroying property, and the list goes on. I just didn't care about anything. I can remember feeling incredibly lonely all the time as I felt like I was in this pit all by myself. Sometime later Stabbing Westward (a late 90's/early 2000's rock band) had a song called "Save Yourself" that had lyrics that went as so; *"My life has been a nightmare; my soul is fractured to the bone. If I must be lonely, I think I'd rather be alone."* I first heard that song in 2000. Those lyrics would bring me to tears when I would look back on the days that I was a troublemaker.

During the winter of that year, my father gathered us kids into the living room in what I always called our "Cracker Box House". We all sat down; my mom in tears. My dad told us that my mother had something to tell us. My mom, I remember vividly, was wearing a robe and looked as if she had recently gotten out of the shower. She was sitting on the left side of the couch. My dad sat on the opposite end. Me, my older sister, my little sister, and my little brother, were all sitting at attention.

My mom started by saying how much she loved us all and then she began to cry. She came out and told us that she had been having an affair. Hysteria reigned supreme in the following moments. Especially from myself. I leaned forward and screamed at my mom. "YOU F#$%&*G WHORE!" which was followed by many other insults. Then I got up and left the house. I got in the car and drove off. I didn't go far. I was gone for about a half hour.

At that point in my life, I was about eighteen years old. I had been in a few relationships where I was head over heels in love with some poor girls who had to become women early in life just to ditch me. Pretty much all of those girls had cheated on me. So that's why I took this news especially hard. Since I was always an introvert, and still am to this day, the thought of betrayal was particularly hard on me. It would blanket over me like the sun ceasing to exist in an instant on a beautiful summer day.

My mom's antics left a dark mark on my life. The woman that raised me, that taught me right from wrong, that was the enforcer for when I was out of line, the one that sat in that attic crying over her Bible and gave her spare time to God was betraying her own family and the scripture she abided by.

Every time I think about those days and those revelations, I always remember my mom sitting in the attic reading her Bible always in tears. Was it the joy of the Lord? The Holy Spirit? Guilt? Repentance? I suppose it was none of my business. As much as I have always wanted to ask, and still could if I wanted to as my mom is still with us, I just assume let her have whatever it is, to herself.

After returning home that night about an hour later, things seemed to have calmed down. On my drive, something hit me like a ton of bricks. My brother! As I walked through the kitchen, my dad was getting a glass out of the cupboard. I asked him, "Dad, what about my brother?"

My dad looked at me and said, "I know Michael." In that moment I knew that my brother and I had different fathers. Adopted, me and my sisters always called my brother adopted or told him he was switched at birth in the hospital when he was a baby because he had blonde hair and blue eyes while we all had brown hair and brown eyes. "All those jokes my sisters and I made about My brotehr being adopted weren't so funny anymore."

I felt like mud.

In a very short period of time, my upbringing became abundantly clear to me. All the fights, the misery, the lack of my parents showing each other love. It all meant something.

Random Preachers

Over the decades I encountered several preachers, ministers, etc. I sometimes got into deep discussion with them when I had the chance to. I had a mental bullet list of arguments that I would make with people of faith. They would always tell me how much God loves me and how I needed to live my life for God. I just didn't buy it. So, I would always ask them questions that led them into oblivion. They couldn't answer these questions which I will get into later and they would always just look at me with an empty defeated look or maybe it was a look of compassion for me.

Their weakness as witnesses made me feel exhilarated about beating God out of my life. I got pure satisfaction out of making someone who had devoted his whole life to God, question his own faith. Even today for all I have been through I still can't answer all those questions, but I do have an answer which you will find at the end of this book. It may not be *the* answer, but it's an answer.

Millions Dying in the Name of Jesus

Learning history in school taught me a lot about the fact that millions of people have murdered in the name of Christianity. It can be hard to hear this type of news and see that it had been happening for hundreds of years and not end up with some kind of question about why it would happen. As time goes on, I have seen many instances whether real or in movies that Christians or believers in God would kill others to prove their point or in trying to force others into belief.

In reading The Bible, I have read that in The Old Testament, God actually supported the killing of others in a fashion of war. Not necessarily because they didn't believe in Him, but because they didn't live right. Without going into depth on this, it is important to know that God did indeed condone war. Jesus, on the other hand, did not seem to condone it. In fact, he urged all his followers to not fight and to not take advantage of one another.

So where did these people get the idea that it was OK to kill in the name of Christ? It seemed to me that The Bible, Jesus, God, was just one giant hypocrisy that wasn't worth the light of day. I mean really, if people are willing to kill *millions* over these words, or ideas then, in my eyes, that was not worth following.

The Many Judges

Over my lifetime, I have been witnessed too many times. When I would protest in the name of logic, I was frequently met with judgement from the witness. They would usually tell me what I needed to do to live my life right under God but there was one problem; he who judges shall also be judged, and yet here they are judging me, doing exactly what The Bible says not to do. I didn't respect that and I deemed them to be hypocrites.

If you are going to tell me how I should live my life by following God's word, then why don't you do that yourself? I can always remember thinking how ridiculous and pathetic these people were. Their approach was generally offensive, annoying, and arrogant.

My battle with Christianity had a long and insignificant impact in my life. It wasn't something that really mattered to me because I didn't believe. I was so sure that God didn't exist that I *knew* I could do whatever I want and there was no price to pay other than that of the price of the law or life. I *knew* that when you died, it was lights out!

The Ex-Girlfriends

Around this turbulent time in my life, I met a girl at a party that I was invited to on a whim. I didn't really know anyone there but on a window seat in the dining room, I was instantly drawn to a girl named Teri sitting there. We talked and I got her phone number. I tried to date this girl, but I didn't seem to be her type. In fact, Teri pretty much told me that I wasn't her type. Over the course of the next year or so, I persisted incrementally. Shortly after the news of my mom, I was thrown out of the house for stealing the car. I stole the car all the time and was caught twice. Second time, I was out!

A few days after I was thrown out of the house, I came back home at about nine o'clock at night. My key didn't work in the door, so I rang the doorbell. My mom answered the door...with the chain on it. Imagine that. She said "Yes?"

"Uh...I live here," I said to which she replied, "No, you don't," and shut and locked the door. I spent about a year or so being homeless. For about six months, I slept on couches at friends' houses. After about six months of that, I ran out of couches to sleep on. I lived in my car. This period in my life was dark. I had no one. All of my troublemaker friends had pretty much turned their backs on me. This girl from the party who I talked to somewhat regularly was constantly on my mind. "If only we were together my life would be better" I would tell myself.

Sometimes, I would break-in to my parents' house and take a real shower. When I couldn't do that, I would find public restrooms that had a slide lock on the door and would bring a towel, soap, and a cup in with me. There, I would rinse myself down with water, lather up, and rinse back off. Yeah, it was awful. But I refused to be dirty. I would park my car in a field down the street from my work, a landscaping company, so that I wouldn't be late. How about that? Homeless, broke, but couldn't handle being late for work! How times have changed.

One morning during the summer of 1995, I woke up and looked out to the horizon. The sun was coming up. I sat there in complete silence and said to myself, "I am not going to die in this car."

I looked around the car and saw the Doritos bags, the 7/11 complimentary cups that had chili and cheese sauce mixed in them for a "real dinner" affect to dip my Doritos into. I said to myself' "I am not going to live in this car either." So I fired my car up and drove thirty seconds to work. That night after my shift, I went and applied for a second job delivering pizza.

I worked and worked and worked. I was close to getting my own apartment and I had about two months of saving to go. It was getting pretty cold at night, so I decided to suck it up and try to go back home. I asked my parents if I could stay there for two months so that I could save a little bit more to get my own place. They gave me thirty days. I was grateful.

After about four months of having my own apartment, Teri and I grew closer, and we started dating. Her brother needed a place to stay, and I offered to let him move in. I had recently been laid off, about two months after I moved in. About two days after being laid off, the engine in my car blew up. I had to get a job at a nearby Arby's, somewhere I could walk to. Once he moved in, we had a great time together even though we hated each other in high school. During this time, we would take some weird pictures. Once we took pictures of us jumping and in midair, we would click the button, so the picture looked like we were flying. Then there were some other weird ones where we took a picture in the kitchen with all of the cabinet doors open.

Over the course of the next four months or so, Teri and I were up and down, in and out. Basically, we were young, and she wanted to go to college and live her life. At the time, I just thought I needed someone to be there for me for the rest of my life, or a soulmate if you will. Eventually, I somewhat manipulated Teri into staying with me. We were together for about four years and got along well.

About two years into our relationship, Teri got pregnant. She insisted that having a child would negatively impact her career. She was working at Progressive Insurance at the time. I wasn't sure what I wanted. At this particular moment, I was grateful for our relationship and wanted to see it last forever. The main thing that discouraged me though was finances. I wasn't good with money and didn't have much, but still, I wanted that baby. In the end, Teri decided to get an abortion. I supported her on the surface but inside, I was struggling immensely. When we went to Planned Parenthood to get the abortion, we sat in the waiting room fairly silent. A few "Are you sure?" moments were exchanged. They called her in, and I stayed sitting in the waiting room. Then I began to pace. I started to get this dark feeling that what we were doing was wrong. After about ten or fifteen minutes, I went up to the nurse and asked them if I could talk to Teri briefly because I wasn't sure we were doing the right thing. I was too late she said. They had already completed the procedure.

As time went on, we began to succeed more in life. In 1999, we bought a nice townhouse and a 1997 Chevy S10 just for Teri. A few weeks later, my friend Daniel and I were driving by a local car dealership when I saw a beautiful Yellow 1980 Corvette sitting in the grass with the T-tops off. I pulled into the lot and took the car for a test drive. I almost instantly "woke up" and realized that I had spent my entire time in Colorado living an insane life that I did not belong in.

As a kid I would walk to school and I would always pass by a house that had a black late 80's Corvette sitting outside that I thought was the fastest car in the world. *Nothing* could top a Corvette! I wanted one so bad and now here I was buying one, and in my early 20's of all things.

Suddenly, NONE of my life fit me, nothing made sense. I bought the car with Teri's dad co-signing for me and my life changed in an instant. That was in May 1999. February 2000, Teri and I were settling into bed. We said our goodnights and just as I was beginning to fall asleep, Teri said to me; "I just want you to know that I am moving out".

I just turned to her, "*Really?*"

So that was that and she moved out a few days later. Teri wanted to get out there and live her life which meant I was FREE. Teri and I were not married but there was an agreement made that when we were done living our lives separately, we would reconvene and spend the rest of our lives together. I am not sure to this day why I thought we were meant for each other in the beginning, but one thing was for sure, I did not feel that way later in our relationship.

I happily accepted her separation announcement and spent the next couple of years having the time of my life. Later on down the road, I felt somewhat guilty that I took her away from the life that she wanted because I realized that I was never really in love with her. It didn't help when I found out that she cheated on me a few months before she left. For a while, we kept in contact until 2002. I was dating a girl named Jackie who I ended up getting pregnant. When I told Teri, she became angry, and our post relationship/friendship ended abruptly.

Unfortunately, my relationship with Jackie was not a pleasurable one. Although we got along and never fought, we also never worked out problems with each other either. We had our daughter in February 2003. In the months leading up to her birth, I was increasingly terrified of having a child to the point that I wished I could turn back time. However, the day she was born changed my life. There is nothing more amazing than holding a baby in your arms knowing that a little person has to rely on you to take care of it and that you created it. It's still terrifying but it's also the most amazing thing in the world all at once.

Jackie and I stayed together for about three years. In April of 2005, I woke up at about 4am to her washing dishes. I asked her why she was doing so at 4 o'clock in the morning and she kept saying "*Nothing.*" After asking several times, I gave up and started heading back to bed. As I turned around and walked away, she said she was leaving me. At that moment, I had decided that, even though she wasn't the one for me, I would stay with her no matter what, for our daughter. There was a strong pull in my mind to beg her to stay for our daughter but my heart just wasn't feeling it. I admit I was willing to let her dictate my future. I knew that staying together was the right thing to do but I was selfish and greedy and allowed her to lead the relationship to an end.

When Jackie left, I was pretty thrilled at the time. It gave me a guilt free "*out.*" I let her go without any argument or fighting. She moved into her own place and, shortly after, her new boyfriend moved in. This made it obvious that she had been seeing this guy for some time before we split. Regardless, the way I saw it...I had my life back!

Teri and I became friends again shortly after my breakup with Jackie. I started spending a fair amount of time with her and found that she had changed immensely. I remember the last time I was close with her she was doing quite a bit of hard drugs, and now she had changed even more!

Teri had been born again! I wasn't sure what to make of that because she seemed very pushy and resentful to what had happened a few years prior. She had told me that she had married the man she had an affair with while we were together. Although she didn't leave me for this guy, she ended up marrying him some time later. She made it a clear point to me for some reason that he was well endowed. I mean, why did I need to know this? She told me she could never have smaller again. Why did I need to know that? So here I am sitting with this

Born-again Christian who tells me she's now pure and wholesome when she suddenly lays this unneeded information on me. Perhaps she wanted me to be jealous? Perhaps it was retaliation for having a child with someone else while she aborted ours. Little did she know that I was not interested in returning to our relationship from the get-go. I'm sure she didn't either. It gets weirder.

She explained her faith to God in great detail and how I need to make the same commitment in my life which at the time, I had zero interest. She made it very clear that she would never have sex before marriage again. So, thinking back a few minutes to the previous part of our conversation, I asked her what she would do if she got married and the guy was too small or not good enough in bed. She then said to me with a straight face, "I don't have to worry about that because God will bless me".

WHOA! This left a huge stain on Christianity for me. I mean, where was she getting this information from? Is this what God promised his people? Since she was such an advocate of The Bible, was that what it actually said? This sounded like the opposite of what God would even care about, and I, at this time, was no Christian.

Needless to say, while I was enjoying having her as a friend again and had hoped to remain friends, in that moment, I had lost a lot of respect for her, and Christians in general.

These moments that I dealt with Christians head on convinced me that God was not real and that if he was, I didn't want to have anything to do with him. If his children are such hypocrites, how could I possibly submit to that way of life?

CHAPTER 6

MAKING MY FAMILY

That same summer, Teri and I hung out frequently. I used to street race almost nightly, or I would go "roll", which simply meant cruising. Sometimes Teri would come with me; even though she wasn't much into it. It was just a part of who I was, and I really didn't care who thought what about me. Except for the cops, I guess. One night we were cruising up Academy Blvd in Colorado Springs which, at the time, had one of the biggest street racing scenes in the country. This was roughly in June of 2005 shortly after Jackie left me. I had recently lost my townhome that I bought with Teri when we were together in a foreclosure. I was back living with my parents and to be honest, I really only cared about cruising around in my Typhoon, work, and dating.

So, as Teri and I are driving along, I notice this red Eagle Talon, TSi AWD up ahead. For the last couple of months, I saw this car everywhere, always going the other way and there was one gorgeous woman that drove this thing. This one time I saw it up ahead and I had a girl with me. Even though she wasn't someone I was dating, it was definitely a buzzkill. Anyway I told Teri, watch this. I punch it and fly past that gorgeous woman setting off the blow off valve right in her ear. It's a part of some turbo cars that makes a loud wooshing sound when you let off the gas. Since she drove a turbo car, I figured she would dig it and, to no surprise, she did!

About a half of a block later she comes flying up on my left with her beautiful brown hair blowing in the wind wearing a wife beater. She yells out, "That's F@#$ SICK!" I just carted myself off like she was no big deal. I turned to Teri and said, "I am going to marry that girl!" Of course, Teri thought that my ego was ridiculous.

A couple of months later, I ran into that same girl cruising around one night. I later found out her name was Michaela. So, I pulled up next to her at a light and asked her if she wanted to ride with me for a while. Michaela said OK, which I was not expecting. We drove around for an hour or two and had a great time. As I was dropping her back off at her car, we were talking about the qualifications we had when dating. Michaela said that she would never date anyone shorter than her. I asked her how tall she was, and she said 5'7". I told her that was too bad because I was 5'6". Well, we started seeing each other anyway and came to find out, I was actually 5'7" and she was 5'6". We moved in together about five months later and got married about two months after that. Even though it was kind of fast, I felt like Michaela was the one for me.

One of the things that made me realize that Michaela needed me was one night we were driving around and stopped at a red light. It was about 1 am. As we were sitting there, she was looking out the window and said, "How do you sell a home?"

I asked her what she meant and she told me that in front of the house on the corner was a "Home for Sale" sign. She told me that you sell a house, not a home. I knew in that moment that she had suffered greatly in her life and that she needed someone to show her that there was a place called home.

As it turns out, Michaela was the right one for me. In fact, we were right for each other. That was sixteen years ago, and we are happier now than we ever have been and it just kept getting better. In the beginning of our marriage, I had a job that I worked because the year before I tried starting my own landscaping business and failed miserably. This was also one of the reasons Jackie left me: money problems. Just before Michaela and I got married, I decided to restart that business.

From then on, the business grew and our lives got better and better over time, however, we always were those people where something always went wrong; it was always some kind of misfortune. For instance, in 2008, I hurt my back really bad. By 2009, I decided to start hiring people which I never wanted to do, but what choice did I have? Landscaping was all I knew. I had no education and knew really nothing else. By 2011, I had two or three employees and was doing mostly commercial and HOA landscape maintenance work. We were slowly growing, both our business and our lives.

As I look back, I still remember mowing that church cemetery in New Jersey as a kid and how I loved the feeling of working outside while seeing the new leaves sprout on the trees in the spring and watching them change color in the fall. I loved the smell of the freshly cut grass and even the smell of the shed where the lawn mower was stored. I loved reading the head stones and hearing the birds chirp while watching the wildlife run around. In a place of death, I was surrounded in life. Mowing that cemetery was the best thing that ever happened to me, and I hold those memories near and dear to my heart to this day and definitely associate my business with my childhood job from back then.

In August of 2012, we had a baby boy named Alexander. He was born a month and a half premature, which meant he was in the N.I.C.U. for a couple of weeks. Once again, I had the unique experience of holding something in my arms who had no choice but to trust in me. He was so adorable in the N.I.C.U. with his little goggles to protect his eyes with those tubes and electronics all over him. I always said he looked like a baby superhero. While, Michaela was constantly worried about him, I wasn't. I knew he would be OK, and he was.

Even though Anjelina, my daughter, spent 50% of the time with her mother, we were still a family. The years we all spent together were absolutely amazing and, while we all certainly had our hard times, I wouldn't trade it for the world. In August of 2021, our daughter went off to the Navy and left us. Even though it left a hole in my life, or as Michaela would say it felt like losing a leg, a strange new chapter was opening.

CHAPTER 7

Finding The Father, The Son, The Holy Spirit, and Dr. Maceo Smith

In 2020, COVID hit. During the first day of the COVID shutdown in Colorado, I had an eerie feeling that something wasn't right about all of it. I couldn't put my finger on it, but I just had this gut feeling that it was the beginning of something that would change our lives forever. As time went on, in-school learning was cancelled and traded for online learning and my wife and I quickly realized that we were not qualified teachers. At least she wasn't, since she was a stay-at-home mom and I really couldn't take any credit for suffering on that front. In the beginning of the 2020 school year, in August, we began to debate if it was a smart decision to continue the public school online learning model for our kids. So, we began to search for other alternatives. We found two charter schools and two Christian schools that we liked. The charter schools were free while the Christian schools we had to pay for. After doing our research, we found that the Christian school near our home was the best option for our children.

Even though it was the most expensive option, we liked their values and morals and, to be honest, it was also very close to home. Unfortunately, our daughter opted not to attend the Christian school. She was seventeen years old and in her senior year. So we decided to not insist that she go and leave the decision to her. Our nine-year-old son, however, was somewhat excited to start that new school year. We never talked about God in our home since we were not religious. My wife believed in God while I did not. I did, however, believe that everyone else should believe in God because as long as the vast majority of the world believed in *something*, it kept people on the straight and narrow.

As our son attended the school, he began to come home from school and say things to me like; "Dad, did you know Jesus said this? Dad, did you know that God said that? Dad, did you know that Jesus did that?"

"Yes," I'd reply every time. I was kind of surprised that I remembered as much as I did. At some point, in the late fall of 2020, my son was on one of his raves about God and I asked him, "Would you like me to take you to church so you can see what these crazy Christian people do?" What? Where did this come from? It was crazy to me because I had never thought of taking him to church let alone asking him if he wanted to go. It just kind of rolled out of my mouth. Funny thing is, ever since I said it, I felt an uncontrollable pull to take him to church.

My son's school was a part of a church I offered to take him to. I always tried to support my kids' beliefs, hobbies, etc. Even though he said he wanted to go, I didn't take him just yet. This event took place roughly in November 2020 and from that day forward, I felt a strong pull to that church. I can't explain it much other than it popped into my head almost every Sunday, Should I go?

Some time passed, and we were in May 2021. At an HOA complex that my landscape company maintained, there lived a man named Dr. Maceo Smith. Dr. Maceo moved to the complex sometime in 2020 and had become the "Landscape Committee". This means that he had direct control and authority over everything our company did on the job site. Dr. Maceo was a tall black man from Texas with a thick country accent. He often wore a cowboy hat and didn't mind getting dirty doing work in the community.

I met Dr. Maceo sometime in the mid-winter, but we didn't really start working together until the spring of 2021 came around. During the month of May, I began to meet with Dr. Maceo somewhat regularly. He would often ask me questions about our Landscape Maintenance Contract and the services that were and weren't included. When he saw something he didn't like or would question me on something in the contract that I would explain and stick to my guns on, he would quote Proverbs 11:3; "The integrity of the upright guides them, but the unfaithful are destroyed by their duplicity."

This drove me insane because I viewed myself as a man with great integrity. For some guy to come waltzing in and suddenly accuse me of not having integrity put me in fight mode. I've had a pretty bad reputation for upsetting clients with my blunt honesty. I was never afraid to tell people what they don't want to hear. I believe wholeheartedly in honesty and accountability. Here is the subject of words again, I heard only one word and that was integrity which I assumed he was accusing me of having none.

An important side note is that during this time, I had watched a movie called "Take Me Home Tonight". It takes place in the 80's and was filmed in 2010. It's a pretty funny movie to say the least and I admit, I do like Romcoms. During the movie, Topher Grace and Teresa Palmer are dancing at a party to the song "Everybody Have Fun Tonight" by Wang Chung. As I watched the scene that I had seen several times before, I realized that I really liked that song, even though I did not care for it as a kid, for some reason now, I felt like it sang to me; I could *feel* it. So, I downloaded it and put it on my thumb drive so I could listen to it in my vehicle. I'll get back to this soon.

In late May, Dr. Maceo, Matt (my Operations Manager), and I were standing out on the west side of the job site which sat on a tall steep hill that overlooked Pikes Peak. It is such a beautiful view, it is as if you could get a good running start, take a giant leap, and fly away over the valley and up to the top of Pikes Peak. We were assessing the job site and planning for the near future. Then we came to a stop and engaged in a more personal conversation. I had thought it to be very unprofessional to talk about religion with clients but since Dr. Maceo led them, I listened and tried not to say anything.

At some point in the conversation, Dr. Maceo said, "God was talking to me the other day..." *Ha, What a goon! This man thinks God talks to him?* I thought.

Matt cut him off and said, "You talk to God?" "

"Yes, I do," Dr. Maceo answered which led to Matt saying, "So, you hear voices." Matt and I looked at each other like we were twelve-year-old boys (I was forty-five and he was fifty-four at the time) and giggled at each other hinting that Dr. Maceo was a little crazy.

Dr. Maceo returned, "I don't hear God here (motioning to his ears), I hear him here (motioning to his torso)." He then asked Matt, "Matthew, do you believe in God?"

"I believe in God, I pray sometimes but I don't go to church or anything like that," Matt responded with a shrug. Dr. Maceo, somewhat rapidly, turned his head to me, "How about you Mike?" He asked in his thick country accent.

"I don't believe in it." I answered. He asked me why. All of a sudden, with no thought I answered, "Because I understand the commitment I am being asked to make and I am not prepared to make that commitment." It just rolled out of my mouth, just like when I offered to take my son to church. Dr. Maceo just smiled at me in a strange way. For some reason, from that point on, that conversation would play in my head at least a few times per week for the next couple of months. It got to be irritating and it burned inside me.

Some time went on and again, Dr. Maceo would pester me in any way possible, seemingly hinting that I wasn't doing my job or doing it correctly. Even worse, I got the impression that he didn't trust me or my people. At every job site walkthrough, I heard; Proverbs 11:3; "The integrity of the upright guides them, but the unfaithful are destroyed by their duplicity." I began to become angry with Dr. Maceo. Resentful in fact. I didn't believe that he really knew what he was talking about as he would frequently tout his business and sales background in alarm systems and landscaping. What he failed to see, in my eyes, was that we weren't landscaping, we were maintaining an HOA complex on a massive scale.

This difference in his and my view set the stage for my severe frustration with this man which led me to be somewhat combative with him. In about June of 2021, Dr. Maceo wanted to meet with me onsite to discuss edging on the property. In our contract, edging was titled as "Sidewalk and Curb Edging". Dr. Maceo had an opinion that edging should be done around all of the gardens between the brick and timber borders and should be a part of the contract. I whole heartedly disagreed. Dr. Maceo did not hesitate to tell me that was how they did it in Texas. I quickly pulled out my phone and said, "OK Google, where am I?"

Google replied, "You are at 1000 Fontmore Rd Colorado Springs Colorado." While listening to the Google Assistant, I looked at him with a big smile on my face and said, "Doesn't sound like we're in Texas, Maceo." He kind of nodded his head and lead me back to his office. When we got there, we pulled the contract out and looked at the Edging clause. Sure enough, it said what I thought. One for Mike!

Fighting, arguing, or even disagreeing with customers is never fun. Even when I was right, they would still feel threatened by this. Dr. Maceo was graceful though. He and I had these disagreements somewhat frequently. I felt that by constantly quoting Proverbs 11:3 that he was doubting or questioning my integrity.

In late July 2021, I become increasingly frustrated with Dr. Maceo because of his professionalism mixed with his faith. The questioning of my integrity was infuriating so I made the decision to go see and confront him about it. When I did sit down with him, I asked him point blank: "Maceo, every time you talk about my contract or my guys' work, you always quote some Bible scripture that talks about integrity. Are you implying that I don't have integrity?"

"No, that's not it, as the Landscape Committee representing my community, I have to make sure that I have integrity when I deal with people like you." Dr. Maceo went on to explain himself. I challenged him a bit as I didn't quite believe him. He became firm in making himself very clear that he only answers to God. What more could I say? I left his office feeling as if there was no resolution and went on about my business.

A couple of weeks later, Dr. Maceo called me and asked me for a proposal on replacing all the irrigation timers on the job site that we had recommended that they do. I spent about six hours on the proposal because he asked me to itemize it which meant that he wanted part numbers and individual pricing. That was something that as a contracting business we did not do. Mainly because a potential client could simply give my proposal that I worked hard on to a competitor and they would have zero leg work to do. That is simply unprofessional and dirty business. I went ahead and did it anyway because Dr. Maceo demanded it. Plus, he was a Christian with good intentions, or at least I hoped.

A few weeks went by and I had not heard anything regarding the proposal. However, Dr. Maceo began to fight me on my irrigation repair bills claiming that all of the ones we sent him were for damages caused by lawn mowers. I explained to him that any heads damaged by mowers were set too high and that they should be lowered and that I would not take responsibility for that. They should pay to have them all set properly which is a time and material job. Dr. Maceo, however, was insistent that he did not approve of some of our invoices.

This guy was driving me nuts. I felt like he was directly taking food off the tables of my people. I didn't think that he really had a clear understanding of how our industry worked. I began to grow extremely angry and resentful of that man and his Bible thumping Christianity. I find that many Christians always seem to expect contractors to work just enough to cover costs.

A few weeks later, I spent about an hour or two reading Bible scriptures on Google. I searched, *"Bible verses about business"* and found hundreds. The first verse I saw was Proverbs 3:27; "Do not withhold good to those whom it is due, when it is in your power to act." I read on and on. After reading about a hundred of them, I came to the conclusion that Proverbs 3:27 made the most sense to the current situation I was dealing with. I set up a meeting with Dr. Maceo the next day. About an hour before the meeting, I began to recite and memorize the scripture. I was on a mission; I was going to blow Dr. Maceo out of the water and back to The Stone Age.

As I arrived at his office, I got this feeling that I should be fully prepared to lose my contract after telling him what I had to say. However, I didn't care; I thoroughly believed I was right. Armed with my Bible verse, I went into the office determined to set this man straight. To my horror, I see on the shelf in his office, eleven irrigation timers. That was it! I'd had enough of this guy. He just made me chamber my round and put my finger right over the big red button. I sat down and Dr. Maceo asked me what was on my mind. I kind of beat around the bush a little bit to feel him out but I kept looking at the shelf which made my blood boil.

Finally, I came out and said it. I told him how irritated I was that he asked me for an itemized proposal so he could go out and buy the materials himself. He had a quick explanation, but

I couldn't hear him in the moment. Then I took the safety off and pulled the trigger, pushing that big red button. "Proverbs 3:27; Do not withhold good to those whom it is due, when it is in your power to act" BOOM! Hiroshima was embarrassing compared to the look on this man's face. *Oh yeah, I got you good Dr. Maceo. What do you have to say about that?* I thought.

Dr. Maceo, with a confused look on his face, leaned back in his forty-year-old office chair at his forty-year-old desk, in the forty-year-old maintenance shed which doubled as an office that smelled like grease, gas, and grass. "What did you just say?" I repeated, Proverbs 3:27; "Do not withhold good to those whom it is due, when it is in your power to act."

"What verse was that?" He asked.

I replied, "Proverbs...3:27, look it up!"

Dr. Maceo with a confused, now possibly angry look on his face says, "Proverbs...3:27, how does it go?"

"Do not withhold good to those whom it is due, when it is in your power to act," I exclaimed. With his hands on the back of his head, he leaned back in that forty-year-old chair and turned to the wall on his left looking at a piece of paper hanging on the wall.

Dr. Maceo said to me in his thick country accent, "Proverbs 3:27; Do not withhold good to those whom it is due, when it is in your power to act. You talkin' about this right here?" Dumbfounded, and terrified, I got out of my chair and walked up to the front of his desk before leaning in to see the paper on the wall. The paper was clean, white, and laminated. It read, "Proverbs 3:27; Do not withhold good to those whom it is due, when it is in your power to act." There it was written in big black letters.

In that very moment, I felt a warming sensation across my entire body with a light coolness on the outside, not like getting sick from food poisoning. Instead, this was shear comfort. I was as light as a feather. Calm and humble. Slowly, I walked backwards until I reached my chair and sat down again. I was in a trance almost. Unsure of what I had just experienced but I could hear Dr. Maceo say, "What made you look that up Mike?"

I told him that I felt like he was doing me wrong and trying to sidestep my efforts which would take money off my employees and my table. He explained to me the financial status of the community and how there were money issues that the board of directors were trying to resolve. He explained this to me over the course of about five minutes while I was still floating so I just accepted what he said. I had no fight in me. I felt free but restrained. I felt comfort but fear. Dr. Maceo, in one second, became something completely different to me than what I previously knew. There was a mystification around him, almost like a fairy tale character. As a die-hard Star Wars fan, I will be honest, he reminded me of Mace Windu. In his looks, confidence, and wisdom.

"Why is that on your wall?" I had asked.

"That's been there almost a year, you ain't never seen that there before?" He asked me and I told him no. "You know somethin' Mike, God speaks to me about you."

"Oh yeah? And what does he say?" I ask quite sarcastically.

"He wants you to be his soldier," Dr. Maceo said with a face as straight as straight could be.

I laughed and asked him , "to do what?" To which Dr. Maceo replied, "To spread his word."

"Spread his word? How am I supposed to do that and why would I? More importantly, what does that even mean?" I asked and then Dr. Maceo went on to explain to me that as Christians it is our primary function in the world to spread God's good word. To bring people to him. I told Dr. Maceo that I was not a believer and never was.

"I don't believe in God Maceo; I never really did."

With his expression the same Dr. Maceo said, "Sure you do Mike; you know you do."

"Oh yeah? How do you figure?" I asked sarcastically. It was hard to buy into what he was saying at first.

"Mike, you remember that day you me and Matthew were talkin' out on that hill? Remember, when I asked you if you believe in God?"

"Yeah." I started to get a little nervous because that day I said what I said was still bugging me, replaying in my mind all the time. Always *pulling* on me.

"You said Mike; 'I don't believe in God because I understand the commitment I am being asked to make and I am not prepared to make that commitment.' Oh yeah Mike, You a believer." I asked him how he came to that conclusion.

"Mike, you used the word 'I' four times in that sentence, you say that you are not PREPARED to make that commitment. That means that you believe, or you at least *know*, but are afraid to commit to God."

I sat there with not much to say. In all honesty, it made perfect sense to me. I began to pry a little; questioning things. I told Dr. Maceo that, since that day on the hill, my response to his question had been replaying in my mind over and over again. Dr. Maceo said, "that's God talkin to ya."

I then proceeded to tell him about how when Covid hit, my wife and I put our son in a Christian school. I told him further that since the day I offered to take him to church, I had felt a magnetic attraction toward it. That something was telling me to go. "God is talkin to ya through your son Mike." Dr. Maceo told me with a serious look. "I think my church is one of the best around but, Mike, you need to go to the church where your son goes to school. There is somethin for you there. God wants you there." I was being receptive to this to say the least. That humble comforting feeling I had was still very present in me.

Our conversation came to an end after about an hour of chatting. When we stood up, Dr. Maceo opened his desk drawer and pulled out a book. It was thick. I thought, *Oh no, please don't give me a Bible!* Then he handed it to me and said, "Ya know Mike, a lot of people pray, but, most don't know how to. This book is called *Prayers That Avail Much*. Read it and practice praying." So, I took the book, opened the cover and saw it had "To: Mr. Mike Lopez From: Dr. Maceo Smith." It was dated, August 18, 2021. Dr. Maceo knew he was going to give me that book that day. The day I came to try to humiliate and shut him up once and for all.

He grabbed my shoulder and my hand and said, "Let's pray."

Begrudgingly, I shut my eyes, bowed my head, and listened to Dr. Maceo pray. That feeling of calmness washed over me again, only this time, it was not only a little stronger but, I started getting teary eyed. Not in a sad way though, it was a more comforting joyous feeling. When the prayer ended, I felt extremely light. On that gorgeous day, as I neared my truck, I had this overwhelming feeling of peace.

I got in my truck and headed up to a property walk with the HOA Board and Matt. We did our walk and afterward, Matt insisted we go to lunch. We met at a nearby Wendy's, but I didn't eat much because I was taking my wife to a special birthday dinner later that night at one of our favorite restaurants. As we ate, I told Matt what had just happened to me. He sat and listened before he commented on how weird it was and I thought the same thing myself.

After lunch, I got in my truck, and started it up. Just as I put my hand on the shifter, the radio began to play. Remember earlier, I had downloaded the song "Everybody Have Fun Tonight", by Wang Chung? I was listening to that song on repeat for at least a few days. Yeah, I'm that guy. Though the song wasn't a favorite of mine as a kid as I stated earlier, something had me stuck on it, the way the music starts and the lyrics, just kind of soothing in a way. I have a pretty deep attachment to music; some parts of some songs can actually make me *feel* something inside me and will move me emotionally, physically and spiritually. I am sure that is the intended purpose for many musicians.

As soon as the music played, the first thing I heard, louder than the engine, louder than any thought I had in my head, louder than the birds chirping outside, was "So Spread the Word!" I became paralyzed for a moment and got the chills with that warming sensation so bad that I literally could not move for a few seconds. Tears were flowing from my eyes like never before. It wasn't sad, but instead it was absolutely amazing! These feelings were so strong that I felt like someone was in the car with me. This event took place no more than two or three hours after Dr. Maceo told me that my job was to spread the word of God.

The lyrics of that verse were:

"Across the nation, around the world
Everybody have fun tonight
A celebration, so spread the word"

This feeling of someone being present in the truck with me was so great that I had to check the back seat. I knew in that moment, that God had just filled me with The Holy Spirit, or had at least talked to me. I didn't even really know what The Holy Spirit was, but I just knew in that moment that was it. God had called me, sitting in a parking lot in a 2007 Trailblazer SS while jamming 80's music. Never in my entire life had I ever felt so terrified and blessed at the same time. They say God works in mysterious ways and they were right: God does.

CHAPTER 8

THE AFTERMATH

Later that evening on the way to dinner for my wife's birthday, I told her about the bizarre events that happened that day. She thought it was weird but didn't say much other than that. The next few days were amazing, I felt incredibly relaxed, comforted and had a great sense of clarity. I was a completely new person. That following Saturday, I had to go to the store and get things for our son's birthday party. At the store, people were driving me crazy. Even worse, when I got back out on the road to run a few more errands, people were cutting me off, giving me "the bird", you know the story. I am not the type to take people's attitudes and have many times gotten into all kinds of road rage incidents which I was not proud of.

By the time I got home, I was a wreck. A few days later, I was back to my old self but I felt incredibly lonely. Abandoned even. I told my wife about it, and she was disappointed and felt bad. Over the course of the following month, I began to think about God constantly. I now knew he was real. So, what now? Well, I didn't know. Toward the end of September, the need to take my son to church was growing in me daily. I started to bring the concept up to my wife and would basically argue with myself, to her, of why I need to go to church. I asked her why it matters if I go to church or not. If I believe and do the right thing, and try to be a good person, then what was the difference?

My wife didn't want to join in on my first trip to church so it was just me and my son. I got a little dressed up and so did my son. We drove our '55 Chevy pick-up truck; my son's favorite vehicle that we own. When we got there, I was expecting a bunch of old people to come running up to me and grab my cheeks while giving me pecks. The closer I got to the doors, the more intense the vision got. I could smell the old lady clothes, the old lady perfume, and I could feel the old lady whiskers with their kisses. I could practically see the old lady clothes, the hats with the dingle berries hanging off the edge, the pastel colors with the white gloves.

As I walked through the doors, I couldn't believe my eyes. No old ladies were rushing to grab my cheeks or kiss me. To my surprise, there was a huge mix of people, all races, all ages, and all types of dress. Everyone was very accepting. A couple of people rushed up to me to introduce themselves and I consider them dear friends to this day.

I walked into the chapel, which was large. It wasn't a mega church by any means but much bigger than most churches I have seen. We sat down and they began to sing. I was a bit uncomfortable because I never liked the singing. My mom would always sing like she was in an opera when we went to church as kids which was so embarrassing. After about twenty minutes of singing, they made a few announcements and then came the pastor. Interesting enough, there was a donation box at the entrance instead of a shiny brass bowl being passed around. Communion was also in a packet, the rice cake thing was in an attached wrapping on top of the grape juice which was in a container looked like a creamer for your coffee. This apparently was a result of COVID.

Soon Pastor Eddie got on stage and began to speak. At first, I didn't think much of the guy. He wore a planal to preach in and spoke in a thick country accent. Overall, he just seemed kind of goofy to me. As I listened to him speak, he talked about how COVID separated us all from each other, how we grew to be even closer to our social media accounts, and further away from each other, and God. He explained how as a people we have lost sense of being around each other for fellowship and in the Bible it says to go to church, for fellowship: **Hebrews 10:25, Acts 2:42, Matthew 16:18, 1 John 1:7, Matthew 18:20, Proverbs 27:17, Galatians 6:2, Colossians 2:2, 1 Corinthians 15:33.**

My question to my wife about why I needed to go to church was answered with a big fat slap in the face. I began to experience that warm and cooling feeling again, ultra-comfort, weightlessness. I felt the Holy Spirit filling me and began to tear up. I submitted to God in that chair and listened on as Pastor Eddie educated us on why we go to church.

I always dismissed church as a way to make money, spread fear to keep people in line, and hide imperfections to pretend we are all going to go to this fantasy land called heaven. (Besides of course going to a boring place to get smooches by creepy old people). As they say, most people that don't go to church don't go because they know someone who goes to church. In this instance, the people that were in the church actually had the opposite effect on me. I actually wanted to stay and get to know a few of them. I didn't though, I split as soon as it was over. My curiosity had been heightened to a level I had not experienced in a long time and I was hungry for more.

I went again the following week with my son. This time, I had several people welcome us back and they were all very gracious and kind. No smooches though. I had a thought this visit would be a waste of time, but I had a *feeling* I was home instead. Although the sermon content of my second visit escapes me, I remember vividly that Pastor Eddie's sermon spoke directly to me resulting in me, once again, being physically filled with The Holy Spirit. Light chills on the outside with a warming sensation on the inside, and a weightlessness with comfort and joy.

I was becoming familiar with this feeling and I was starting to crave it. I was craving The Holy Spirit, the word of God, fellowship. My life was changing faster than it ever had in my life, except maybe for the move from Jersey to Colorado. The difference in this situation was that the Holy Spirit urged me on this path. My heart was open for a split second and The Holy Spirit rushed in and grabbed my spirit. It took a lot of courage to do this because of my beliefs and I certainly didn't want to admit to others that I had been wrong.

I fit right in at church for the most part. I truly believe it was just the right church with amazing people and an amazing Pastor who I consider a friend today. My initial thought was to try out five to ten churches before settling on one but, as it turned out, there was no need. I picked the right church for me and what a bonus, it just happened to be where my son went to school. The Holy Spirit is amazing, no?

The one thing I was not expecting to come out of going to church was to like anyone there, but I love these people. They were an amazing group led by an amazing Pastor.

On the third week, my wife started going with us. As we were getting ready to go, we got into a huge fight about something so silly I couldn't even remember what it was. She drove us there and on the way the fight got worse and worse. When she pulled into the parking lot, I was about to explode. So, I jumped out of the car and walked home. I refused to go into this place in such a bad mood. When she came home a while later, she was calm, and we got along. When I asked her what that day's sermon was about, she told me it was about resolving issues in your marriage and how important it was in the eyes of God.

She seemed to enjoy it. Since then, we have gone together almost every Sunday. When Halloween rolled around, one of the church members who was the first to talk to me when I started going invited my family and I out to lunch after the service. We accepted the invite and, when we went, we talked about my coming to Jesus. I told Gary and Skip how excited I was and that I was reading The Bible on Audible.com. Gary asked me where I was in my reading and I told him Genesis. Yup, I was determined to read The Bible from page one to page five thousand. Yes sir, I was on a roll.

Gary advised me not to read The Bible from cover to cover. He suggested I start with Matthew, Mark, Luke and John. Then I could read on. At first I thought Gary was wrong. Why start in the middle of the book? So, Gary asked me, "If you lived in a foreign country and you were going to move to America, would you start reading American History from page one to present day? Or would you start by reading The Constitution? I didn't even have to think about it; "The Constitution!" I replied.

I went ahead and finished Genesis because I was more than halfway through but since Gary gave me a Bible, donated by another church member to me by a great man named Steve Leaming, I went ahead and started to read Matthew, Mark, Luke and John. I was amazed at how much I actually learned about Jesus. I always found it interesting how so many non-believers slammed The Bible without ever actually reading it. Myself included. I always made comments about how contradictory it was; not even having ever read it in any depth, always going off of what other people told me.

The truth is, I had no idea if The Bible contradicted itself or not. I don't claim to be a Bible wiz, expert, or even someone who really knew much about it in any depth. In reading the Gospel, I had learned how we are supposed to live and how we are supposed to treat each other. I finally understood why Christians talked to us non-believers the way they do, with the passive-aggressive threats of hell, why the way we dressed and the language that came out of our mouths was so unacceptable.

Even though I finally understood, I am still reminded of how much I've always hated the judgement, the crossed eyes, and the head shaking. It was belittling to say the least and while I can't speak for others, I can say that it never made me want to be close to God, no, it made me want to destroy God and those who believed. I spent decades of my life discounting and trying to disprove God's existence. Like many others as you know. If our primary function is to spread the word, then maybe it is time for a change on how we do so.

CHAPTER 9

The Law

Growing up, I was devious, rebellious, and extremely independent. When we moved to Colorado, I got into a lot of legal trouble. By the time I was seventeen, I had been arrested multiple times and had been to juvi. I was mostly arrested for theft and had a menacing charge as well. By the time I was eighteen, I had picked up a few more thefts, assault, and harassment charges. I plead guilty to all of them.. Looking back on these incidents, I was being held accountable and had accepted it. I didn't have much of a choice because I couldn't afford the lawyer to get me out of it at the time. The one charge I had received that I plead *not* guilty to was the harassment charge.

It was about September if I remember correctly, I had just gotten home from school and decided to make some spaghetti. As I was stirring the sauce and letting the water boil, my brother came rushing in the front door yelling "Mike, these two guys down the street said they were going to shove his steel toe boots up my a**!" A switch then went off. My newfound pleasure in beating people senseless was finally being put to good use by defending my family.

I told my brother, "Stir my sauce, I'll be back!"

I grabbed an aluminum shaft that was from my old lacrosse stick. The handle was wrapped with athletic tape for good grip. I admit, I fully intended on using this shaft to possibly put the guys out of commission for a while. I ran down the street and as I neared the intersection where my brother said he was threatened, I saw my little sisters' friend, Amanda. She was yelling at the two guys, so I asked her which one it was. She pointed to the smaller guy. From where I was standing, he looked to be about my height, maybe a smidge taller, and kind of skinny. The other guy looked to be about 5' 10" and heavy set. I decided I wasn't going to need the bar and handed it off to Amanda asking her to hold it for me until I was done.

I ran down to them and pushed the culprit. I head butted him lightly and started telling him to hit me. I also mentioned that he had just threatened my brother and now he was going to have to pay the price. As I was in his face, I kept yelling "Hit me, hit me!"

Finally, he asked why and I snapped, "So, I can knock your @$$ out!"

Never in my life had I wanted to hurt someone so badly. I admit, I wanted redemption from when my brother and I were kids. His mom came out of the house and it turned out we were in his front yard. She started yelling at me and we had a nasty verbal altercation.

She yelled "Shelby, get in the house, call the police!"

Then I went home and forgot all about it. The next day, after school, I was hanging out downstairs in my room yapping to some girl on the phone who I had a crush on when the doorbell rang. I went upstairs to see it was the cops. I opened the door. After I hung up the phone and they asked for Michael Lopez. I told them I was he. They arrested me and gave me a court summons for harassment. I couldn't believe it. All I did was defend my brother. When I told my parents, they were not as upset as I thought they would be.

When my arraignment came, I plead not guilty. Hmm, now isn't that interesting. I committed a crime, I knew I did but I plead not guilty. Why? Because in my mind, I was right to do what I did on a moral level. I was defending my brother, his honor, my family's honor. My parents even hired an attorney to defend me. Just six months earlier, I had been arrested at my house for bike theft. Just as the cops were about to pull away, my mom pulled up and asked what was going on. When the cops told her, she yelled "Lock him up, get him out of my sight!"

Funny thing is, the cops told her that they were not taking me to jail. Funny at the time anyway, looking back, my mom was simply tired of my antics.

When my day in court came around, I got to watch the testimonies of all the people involved. It was interesting to see how people lied. Shelby said he was afraid for his life. That was interesting considering we were about the same size and I offered for him to hit me first, not including the fact that he had a much bigger friend with him. Andrea made it clear that when I asked her to hold the bar she refused. I am sure she just didn't want to get in trouble. Understandable. But the worst part was Shelby's mother. She sat on that stand practically in tears acting like she was terrified that I was going to hurt her. It was amazing because of how aggressive she was the day of the altercation, but to be fair, she was defending her son like I was *defending* my brother. I think I was the only one who told the truth that day.

I can remember vividly glaring at her with my lawyer nudging me constantly and writing on the tablet, *"Look like the victim, Look scared, Look sad,"* but I couldn't bring myself to do it; I was defending my brother; *I was justified*. Right? As she gave her testimony, any rational thought escaped me. The thought of winning or losing the case was completely irrelevant; I just wanted blood. I was so angry I thought my head was going to explode. I kept imagining myself jumping over the table and beating the mom and judge senseless because I was cornered and lost.

When the trial came to an end, about an hour or two later, the verdict came in. I remember sweating, kinda shaky even. As the judge read, I felt a nausea coming on; would I go to juvi? Would the judge see that this guy started the whole thing and that his mother was a liar? What would I get if I was guilty? Jail? Probation? Public execution? The judge stated his finding, "I find the defendant, guilty of harassment." I was now enraged. I fixed my *glare* on to the judge. He went on with his end of trial speech and then asked me, "Mr. Lopez, do you have anything that you would like to address to the court?"

I looked down at the table for about two seconds then looked at him and said, "Yes, your honor I do, if it were your brother, what would you have done?"

The judge looked me dead in the eye for about five seconds. I remember how blue his eyes were and how straight his face was. All I could think to myself was how I was right in what I did. I defended my brother's honor. Finally, the judge proclaimed, "Mr. Lopez, I would have done the same thing but, unfortunately for you, you got caught and **the law is the law**."

He smacked his gavel on the pedestal and that was that. I guess I wasn't the only one to tell the truth that day. I was devastated.

As time went on, I was extremely resentful of "The System". I spent time in juvi, went to jail, and got into all kinds of trouble with my then *friends*. What I came to learn eventually was that the law *was* the law. I realized that it didn't really matter what my morals and values stood for; it mattered that I broke the law. It was a very difficult lesson to learn and I still struggle with it to this day sometimes. Learning to fight when I was a teenager taught me to always stand up for myself, especially against bullies. When someone does me wrong, I still have that fight mentality inside me. I tend to lust for the feeling of my fist against someone's face who had disrespected me or a loved one. It wasn't because I enjoyed fighting or hurting people, it was because I learned long ago that one of the only ways to get a point across or shut someone up was with violence.

Violence was huge in my life as a young man. Since I was a short guy, I was picked on a lot and found I was frequently defending myself against people bigger than me. I suppose one could say that I was trained by society to be mean, direct, and heartless. Since I always had to fight people bigger than me, it made me realize that if I stood my ground I would always be victorious even if I lost because I was always the underdog. At least that was how I saw it back then. It took me decades to understand that the law was not exactly about morals and values, it was about breaking the law. The law was designed to keep man safe and prevent people from being taken advantage of.

That doesn't mean the law was wrong. In fact, after reading Matthew, Mark, Luke, and John, I realized that so much of our society and culture was built on the words of Jesus, God, and The Bible. Jesus says, "If anyone slaps your right cheek, turn your other cheek to them as well." That was a tough pill to swallow. Of course, it is important to understand the context of all scripture but what I am trying to convey here is that God spoke the law, Jesus spoke the law.

Once I felt The Holy Spirit, I knew God was real, I had not a single doubt in my mind. Once I accepted that, I then started asking what was the point of feeling The Holy Spirit? Why me? What was next? That of course was what brought me to church. By reading Matthew, Mark, Luke and John as instructed, I realized that what I was really reading, was the law.

As I read, I began to understand what my purpose in all of this was, why God spoke to me, why I was filled with The Holy Spirit. When Dr. Maceo said that God spoke to him about me, he told me that God said he wants me to be his soldier. When I asked, "To do what?" He replied, "To spread his word." Hmm. The song said, "So spread the word!" I realize as I read through the good book, that God not only wants me to spread the word, but he wants all of us to spread the word, and be obedient of course.

Since God told me to spread the word through strange methods, I knew that spreading the word had to become my primary focus in life. As a local owner of three businesses, where would I find the time? Strangely, I started doing things to learn more about The Lord. I started going to a Bible study before church service, Bible study Sunday evenings, and I joined a Christian men's group and fellowship. This had consumed my time and taken me somewhat away from my businesses, but I also feel more productive as I was motivated in my day to get more done and faster so that I could devote more time to God.

I generally started my day at 4 am and was usually at my office by 4:30 am. I read my confessions out loud which took roughly ten minutes, then I read my Bible anywhere from ten to forty minutes, depending on how much time I had left. I started reading The Bible in November, at the time of writing this book. It's now April and I will be reading 1 Peter tomorrow. I don't say that to brag, I'm just that hungry for the word. Reading The Bible has opened my eyes to the truth about The Bible, God, and Jesus.

So many people insult God, The Bible, and have never really even taken the time to read it as I said earlier. So many people take the word and rearrange it to suit their own needs. So many people, claim that you don't have to do this or, you don't have to do that because that was all two thousand years ago. As long as you have a good heart that is all that matters.

My friends, I am here to tell you, that is NOT all that matters. There are real commandments that we are to follow with real consequences. I spent the majority of my life being a non-believer because I couldn't accept that God would cast us into the fiery pits of hell for sinning when sinning is in our nature. Talk about being set up to fail. I couldn't accept that there were so many diseases in the world if there was a God that loves us. I couldn't accept that God would turn his back on innocent people who did not deserve to die for nothing. How could I possibly submit to a God that had no problem allowing me to be poor, live in my car, and be picked on for being short?

Just remember: the law is the law.

CHAPTER 10

How Christians Need to Treat Non-Christians and Why It Is So Important to Christianity

It pains me to say to you that the law is the law and that we have to follow it, not to be saved, but because we are saved. I would love nothing more than to tell you that you will be just fine as long as you are a good person. I wish that was good enough. It is this pain that I endure that encourages me to write this book and put it into your hands, and you hopefully read it and at least consider what I am saying to you. Why does this pain me? Because I had spent my entire life being a non-believer and now that I know what I know, this is going to be a serious challenge to wake people who were like me up and guide them to the truth.

This is something that I have been charged with by God. I can't really say that I am qualified for the job, but I know why God chose me to do this job the way I am doing it. It's because of the languages that I speak, the "tongue". You see, as someone who has been and done so many things, I have seen and dealt with so many people that I have learned at least three languages, besides the English, or a cultural or ethnic language. How about that aye?

As a troubled teen, I learned the ways of the street. I learned the struggles that people go through on a daily basis. As a former athlete, I learned what it was like to experience glory, perseverance, and humiliation. As a worker, I learned what it meant to do an honest day's work and make very little in return. As a business owner, I learned what it meant to be greedy, to take advantage of people, to have to use persuasion on a constant basis. As a manager, I have had to learn to communicate with people on a professional level and talk to them in a manner of respect that I did not always think they deserved.

It is in these experiences that I have realized why I matter; it is to write this book. It is to minister with this book. If I don't make any money from this book, I am OK with that. I am writing this book to reach YOU! I can see YOU sitting there in your tent under the bridge, I can see YOU sitting there in your halfway house, I can see YOU sitting in your house with the sun shining through your favorite window while drinking your coffee, I can see YOU sitting there in the bookstore asking yourself; "Who does this guy think he is?" Yes I am talking to YOU.

Everyone can benefit from this book. Not just people who are on the fence about their belief, not just people who already believe, but anyone. As Christians, we have to start watching how we minister to non-believers and on the fencers. So how can we do that? That is where speaking in different tongues comes in; other languages within your language. Speaking in the different ways I listed earlier is a start. The main idea here is that everyone is different and there is no right way to reach someone who isn't sure. Everyone receives information differently therefore the more internal languages that you can speak the better the chance you have of reaching people with the word.

If you recall, I hated Christians because of the way they ministered to me. People were forceful, judgmental, and oppressive. Last Sunday, I went to my parents' church in Colorado Springs for a mass. My family and I went with them because they had gone to our church a few times and we thought it was the right thing to do. Like I said earlier, I grew up in Catholic and Episcopal churches, though frankly I don't see a difference in the two because they seem very much the same to me. But I looked closer this time. My recent coming to The Lord has changed the way I see everything in life, especially, church.

As I walked into my Parents' church, I looked around at the inside which was built in 1873. I recounted once more the sixty foot ceiling, the beautiful stone pillars, the prayer candle stations, the stained-glass stories, the old wooden pews, and the smell of a church. I looked around at all of it and took my seat, just taking in its beauty. Yet, as I sat there I noticed something else, something not so beautiful.

That week I had finished reading in The New Testament all the way up to Jude. Revelation was next. I had been forewarned by a few friends from my church not to take Revelation lightly; I was told to re-read The New Testament *before* tackling Revelation. I decided instead, to go ahead and read ALL of the study notes I had in my study Bible. Throughout my reading of The New Testament, two things became abundantly clear to me. 1. So much of our way of life, requirements, etc., in the world comes straight from The Bible. 2. Where do churches get their ceremonial traits from? Everything I had ever seen in church; I had NOT seen in The Bible.

Revelation is the key here. I noticed some obvious differences between my church and theirs. The Episcopal and Catholic Churches are extremely ceremonial. When I read Revelation, I found that the twenty-four Elders seemed to pray in a chant like manner. In reading Revelation, I connected a lot of dots to the way the Catholic Church conducts their masses; everything was dark, dreary, drab, depressing, and scary. I am going to step out on a limb here and even say, oppressive. In reading Revelation, I got the impression, at a glance, that maybe this is how church was supposed to be. I can tell you that as I looked around the room, I didn't see a single smile on any face of the attendees, with the exception maybe of when everyone shakes hands and says "peace be with you."

Was that the way we are supposed to live as Christians? Was that how we are supposed to treat each other? Was this how we are supposed to worship? As a new Christian, I don't feel qualified to answer these questions but I can tell you this, I certainly do believe that if we want to bring people to the lord we surely will not succeed in doing so by beating people down verbally and emotionally. Of course, my point is not that we should make Christianity less than what it is by easing Jesus' expectation and requirements, but we can certainly show people that love and happiness exists in God and that you can live a happy life as a believer and a *servant*.

Servant, why does that word seem harsh? No one, especially non-believers, *want* to be considered servants, especially in this country and in our current culture. No one *wants* to be sheep, yet we all are no matter what we do. I am reminded of all the times I would come to a red light, and you would see ten cars in the left, right or middle lane but none in the other lanes.

"SHEEP! Look at all these Sheeple!" I would yell. "Look right there, that Sherson is such a follower!" I would yell these things in my car to myself or whoever might have had the pleasure of riding with me as I picked an empty lane, went and worked seventy hours a week to live a decent life, all in the name of not being like everyone else.

I worked so that I could provide a good lifestyle for my family, so that we could be in good health, and that I could have all of the things that I wanted. All my life, I was so concerned with myself and my accomplishments that I never saw any way possible to ever credit anyone else with my success, especially God. I have always known that God gave us free will. So even at the few times when I had questioned my belief, I knew that God did not play any part in what I did except for what was bad. I could blame God for everything bad in my life but never could credit God for anything good. My personal belief is that God stays out of our business except for in small ways like guiding our paths. It is ultimately up to us to take his instruction and perform the *action* that he wants us to. All I am saying here is that I don't believe that God gives us that promotion, wins us the lottery, or keeps our car from running out of gas when we are in the middle nowhere.

Accountability for our actions is huge. As a business owner, it is my job to hold people accountable for their actions whether it is good or bad. This is one of the languages I have had to learn to speak, accountability. In a society where accountability and common sense are dying, I view it as a language; a language that sadly many people no longer speak. It goes back to "the law is the law". If we don't live by God's law, God's word, then we are held accountable. Interesting enough, as I read The Bible I can see how much of our society has been built around God's commands and Jesu teachings. In the end, accountability is everything.

Even Christians who mean well by ministering to non-believers or on-the-fencers are accountable to their actions, even if they treat a non-believer or an on-the-fencer poorly. This is because we are NOT above them. So many Christians make this cruel mistake. We are to love our neighbors as we love ourselves. One problem I have seen is that many people don't really love themselves. I always thought it was strange the saying; "You can't love someone else until you learn to love yourself." Yet, it makes a lot of sense to me now. So, what are many Christians doing wrong?

Christians are not taking the time to truly understand the mindset of a non-believer or on-the-fencer. Why not? Maybe because most don't care. There is an inherent attitude amongst many Christians that we are somehow above those that don't believe. There are some scriptures that tell us to eject non-be-lievers and sinners from our lives and yet Jesus also tells us to love one another. It is very important of course to remember that we have to understand the context of scriptures that we read in our Bibles. Non-believers and on-the-fencers see this in us and often times associate The Good Lord with our hypo-critical imperfections. So, now is the time to change.

To truly understand the mindset of a non-believer and an on-the-fencer, let's dig in and ask ourselves, what are their primary reasons for not believing in God or being skeptical in the first place? First off, our non-believing neighbors are often very logical people. There is something to be said for logic in this world so we have to be careful when we minister to these folks because they will make some *very* good counter points. I spent forty-five years making these arguments with friends, family, and strangers before I came to The Lord. Let's start at the beginning, shall we?

Dinosaurs

Some might argue that The Bible mentions nothing about dinosaurs. Why would it? No one was around to write about them and what purpose would God have to mention them? Why create them, then? We will touch back on this shortly.

Adam and Eve

Many people question the existence of Adam and Eve. How could there have been two people that just appeared one day? Although The Bible explains this, it is often viewed as a far-fetched concept which leads us to...

Evolution

This one used to get me because we have scientific evidence to some degree as to where we come from.

However, did it ever occur to anyone that, since God created the earth in six days, a day to God is a billion years? Did anyone ever think that maybe we are byproducts of God's earth? That perhaps God took note of us and decided to roll with it and see where we would go? Just a thought. This theory could explain the rise and fall of dinosaurs and prehistoric animals. Again, just a thought. I am no expert on the matter but it's something I have wondered from time to time and have argued about with believers for decades.

The Bible is Contradictory and Written by Man

The Bible was indeed handwritten by man, some of it passed down verbally. It is said, however, that The Bible was written by men under the influence of The Holy Spirit. Just saying "The Holy Spirit" out loud to non-believers sounds silly to say the least. Most people tend to think you are insane if you say that The Holy Spirit told you something. Since The Bible was written by man, it is often dismissed because man is greedy and imperfect so therefore not trustworthy. I always thought that The Bible was written to create fear in people so that they might be controlled. One interesting concept regarding the view of Biblical contradictions is that science is also man made, as for the processes we use to calculate, discover and so on. It is not to say that science is wrong, but it certainly has been.

So, man would rather rely on himself than God. A view that I once held myself. There is no doubt about it; faith can be very trying and quite frankly discouraging. Furthermore, many claim that since

The Bible was written by man, it has been changed and translated over the centuries. In knowing this, how can you possibly take it as truth?

I read the NIV Bible and often other translations when they are present. I can see why people would make this argument; however, the different translations were made in order to help people understand what they are reading better. All in all, based on what I have seen, they all say pretty much the same thing. The same point is essentially made. The King James Version is the oldest produced version of The Bible (I don't know for a fact that this is true) and accepted by many as genuine. Although, it is also very hard to read for the simple man. Again, they all dictate the same message.

All of this said, the actual history of the Bible is extensive and quite intriguing. It is important to understand history itself and how people work when researching the origins of The Bible. Furthermore, when people refer to The Bible as contradictory, it can more or less show a person's lack of knowledge of scripture and context. Let's be realistic, it's a lot of reading and it's easier to be dismissive if you haven't read it in its entirety, no less study it.

If God is Real, Why Are There Other Religions That Started on Other Sides of the World?

This was always one of my favorite arguments. Think about it, while Jesus was being persecuted, on the other side of the world, Buddhists were praying in their own temples. In fact, they had been praying in their temples for two to three thousand years.

Additionally, at that time, the Mayans were going strong and apparently nearing their end. They were worshiping Kukulcan, Itzamna, Ix Chel, and many others. The Romans in the area, of course, were worshiping their own gods similar to the Greeks. So, who is to say that any of them were right?

Believe it or not, The Bible covers this in Genesis when it talks about The Tower of Babel. It is a tough story to swallow, for sure. I never bought it and when I came to The Lord and read Genesis, I took it as truth for a reason that I will get to later.

Why Did God Not Expose Himself to the Entire World?

Another one of my go-to questions when I was up against a tough believer. Let's break it down. In The Bible, God charges us all with living life by his word and spreading his word. If that is the case and God really wants us to do this, then why didn't he expose himself to the rest of the world? What happens to those who were not exposed? Are they judged? Did God only care for the Israelites? Did he only care for The Jews? When God sent Jesus to die on the cross, did he die for the whole world? Why would he need to if people on the other side were clueless to his existence and had their own Gods? At what fault would they be? The whole thought always seemed unfair and hypocritical to me.

After reading the entire New Testament, I have found that God does not really interfere with our affairs. What God does is give us spiritual strength and wisdom so that we may make our decisions based on *his word*. Nowhere in The Bible have I read that he will keep anyone or anything from death to prove his existence or otherwise. In fact, God is NOT to be tested.

This is still a subject that I grapple with.

Why Does God Let Babies Die?
It is not that he *lets* babies die, it's that babies die. Just like people get cancer, get hit by cars, shot in grocery stores or in schools. God does not play a hand at this. Christians and non-believers have got to start to realize that God gave us all free will. This means, *we* make decisions for ourselves, and we have to deal with the consequences when we are held accountable. I am not trying to be insensitive; it just seems clear as day to me when I read the word. People have a bad habit of making up what the word says and again, never actually take the time to read and *understand* what they are reading.

No God That Loves Me Would Let Me Suffer
Why not? You have free will, and his job is to love you. Do you understand that loving you means loving your *spirit*? Your spirit is not your body; your spirit resides in your body (or as Dr. Maceo would say, "Your Earth Suit") until you expire. So, when people watch their loved ones suffer when they were a good person and didn't deserve their suffering, know that God didn't necessarily bring their suffering on them.

Here is a harsh thought, did you love God as much as he loved you? You were supposed to. Let's just say you did; does that mean you will have a great life on earth? Not necessarily. All you have to do is read the word to find out how it all works. My mission is not to write the word here but to guide you to it so that you can see for yourself.

If we are led by ignorance, then we will be ignorant. The truth is written, and it is available for you to read.

God is Selfish – He Wants Me to do What?
God clearly lays out his requirements for us to spend eternity with him. The question is, *why* do we have to be so good, so righteous, so sinless? The answer is quite simple. If God doesn't know sin and he wants us to spend eternity in his Kingdom, why would he want people (spirits) who do not have him in their hearts? I don't get the impression that Heaven is a free for all or a place where you get to do anything you wanted to do on earth but couldn't. Heaven is a place where you feel no pain, no sorrow, no hunger. Where you feel love and comfort from God. If you have never felt God's love before, this will be a tough concept for you to grasp. Feeling God's love is like nothing I have ever felt in my life. I always thought going to Heaven and spending all day worshiping God was lame. Truth is, I had no idea what we do in Heaven. To some degree, I still don't but I don't really care either.

So, imagine that you had a store that sold produce and all the farmers in the area wanted to sell you their lettuce but most of it was partly brown. You aren't going to buy that are you? You wouldn't try to sell that to your customers, would you? Now with that said, from my reading, The Bible doesn't say a whole lot more about Heaven other than it is paradise. The Greek translation of Paradise is The Park. Remember, I am new at this so forgive my ignorance about what Heaven is.

What I feel quite qualified to say is that it sounds a whole lot better than being dead for eternity or burning in hell. As boring as Heaven used to sound to me, now that I have felt God's love, I can't imagine being without it.

So, is God selfish because he wants us to worship him and hang out in the park for eternity? I think not, he is offering you eternal life! What is selfish about that? He is willing to give you eternity in Paradise and you are only willing to give him skepticism? It sounds like we are the selfish ones.

I Don't Believe in Fairytales: The Bible

So many people view The Bible as a fairy tale. I used to as well. The main reason for this, I believe, is because many Christians refer to The Bible in a fairy tale like manner by the way they speak of it. When in all actuality, The Bible is an instruction manual that is meant to be taken seriously. It is so much more than just a story. When reading Revelation, I formed lots of pictures in my mind as to why people would view The Bible as a fairy tale. After all, there are a lot of images that are presented to you in a way that many fairy tales are told.

I cannot imagine that, if your heart is open to God, you could read The Bible as a fairy tale. I believe that the vast majority of people who make this claim have never bothered to pick the book up and read it. There are a few scriptures that show quite a bit of validity in The Bible. For example, **2 Peter 3:14-16 – "Bear in mind that our Lord's patience means salvation, just as our dear brother Paul also wrote you with the wisdom that God gave him. [16] He writes the same way in all his letters, speaking in them of these matters. His letters contain some things that are hard to understand, which ignorant and unstable people distort, as they do the other Scriptures, to their own destruction."**

Think about this for a minute, if The Bible were a planned, conspired fairytale, do you really think a scripture like this would be in it? Here is another one, Paul writes in **2 Thessalonians 2:17, "I, Paul, write this greeting in my own hand, which is the distinguishing mark in all my letters. This is how I write."** Not convinced? How about this one? **2 Timothy 4:11-13, "Only Luke is with me. Get Mark and bring him with you because he is helpful to me in my ministry. [12] I sent Tychicus to Ephesus. [13] When you come, bring the cloak that I left with Carpus at Troas, and my scrolls, especially the parchments."**

In my reading I found similar scriptures that told me this was no planned conspiracy, or a fairy tale, like in Acts 20:7-12 when Eutychus fell asleep and fell out of the third story window because Paul "went on and on". The men that authored these books was convicted in what he was writing. Otherwise, what purpose would these writings have in The Bible? Or any other book for that matter. And as far as who wrote what, man or God himself, remember, *we* are the ones being tested of our faith, not Him. What this means is that God gave us free will. He wants to know that we will follow him and have faith in him without proof. However, here and there you get these little tid-bits of evidence.

Science

First, let me be clear that I do believe in science. Although I do not think that there is anything to believe in, there are simply facts that science has proven. Funny thing though, science has, in many instances, made claims to have discredited The Bible. While Biblical scholars in turn have claimed to have discredited science. I have read countless articles regarding science disproving The Bible and vice versa. What I have found is they both make believable arguments. In regarding science, humans have had to have an explanation for everything, and they have succeeded very well in discovering God's secrets along with exposing them. However, let us ask this question; if science is correct, does that negate God? What has science done to truly disprove God? You can believe in The Big Bang Theory, but you can't believe in God? I will come back to this and the other arguments with one simple response; once you've felt the Holy Spirit, it does not matter.

People See Religion As Divisive or Non-Inclusive

If you look through history and even in current times, you can see that religious extremists will kill for what they believe in. That's right, people will kill for God. A complete and total hypocrisy in it of itself. It is in this extreme condition that non-believers can make an instant decision that God isn't worth the trouble because someone decided to kill in His name. Kings and Queens along with

Presidents and Dictators have banned The Bible in history for this very reason.

Ask yourself this: If someone killed in *your* name when you told them that you just wanted them to love everyone as themselves, how would that make you feel? To all the narcissists out there, we know, you would be flattered. However, that isn't how God feels. So, people take it upon themselves to discredit or reject God because of a decision that was made by an extremist. Therefore, God is divisive or not worth the headache in the eyes of many.

As far as inclusion goes, many people feel as though they have no place in a church; even if they are believers. Many people feel that they will not be accepted when they walk through the door. Sadly, many of these people are right. So the question begs, is Christianity divisive and non-inclusive? No, my friends, it's the PEOPLE that are. What are Christians? PEOPLE. People who believed that Christ died for our sins and was resurrected.

On many levels, Christians are both divisive and non-inclusive; hypocrites if you will. Do not be that Christian. Treat people how you want to be treated and if you say that you wouldn't be how they are in the first place, know that it doesn't matter! That person will never come to God if everyone who represents God treats him or her in a negative manner. We are supposed to be his representatives, his light, his city built on a hill that can't be unseen. So, act like it!

People See it as Brainwashing

I can admit it does partially sound like brainwashing. If you sit in a church and listen to the priest, pastor, minister, whatever, many will talk to the congregation in a manner that sounds judgmental, condescending, or controlling. It is in these types of ministers where brainwashing becomes a focal point to the non-believer and as they listen to their controlling, judgmental, condescending, brainwashing sermons, they pass along to their friends and peers what they have learned.

Remember that in business, people will tell ten other people about their bad experience but someone who has a good experience might tell two people. As representatives of God, we must keep this in mind so that the fragile might not be dissuaded. When you tell someone something repeatedly with the intention of *changing* their mind, that is essentially brainwashing. Do not do that.

When attending a church, insist on a church that encourages you to eread The Bible. Any that don't clearly do not want you to read the truth for yourself.

Why Do Bad Things Happen to Good People?

This is a good question. Many people know of good solid Christians that live with bad fortune. I also know some personally. This can be quite unfortunate. These people, in my opinion, have a few issues. One, they can show the world that they are devout Christians, but they may be sinning when no one is looking. Remember that a man's actions can be judged by what he does when no one is looking. Do you think you can hide the truth from God? Two, just because you are *obedient* to *God's* word doesn't mean that *you* will make all of the right decisions. Some people are just bad with money, life, and decision making. They have to take accountability. Just because you are true to God does not mean he will do everything for you, you have to get out there and make things happen. You have to make the right decisions. God does not work for you; you work for him!

Another issue is Satan. I always thought that the idea of Satan was corny and foolish, fairytale like if you will. I actually had a talk with a friend one afternoon about Satan. He told me that he does not believe there is a Satan and that God is the one who tests you. Although my friend is not a believer, he is still a great man.

However, in my walk with God I've noticed that when someone is a strong believer, Satan will absolutely challenge their faith. When I am doing well with putting God first, that seems to be when bad things start to happen and when I end up in altercations with people that I wasn't looking for. I cannot explain in any terms when it happens. I feel lost, alone, and like God has forgotten me. I have been training myself to identify those moments and pray. To confess and double down on my faith and my relationship with God.

I work hard to overcome those moments because Satan wants me to feel abandoned. However, I push through and feel God's love. It is worth it to have the patience because of the reward received after preserving to feel God's love once more. Make no mistake about it, Satan will give you a seemingly innocent hand to set you on the wrong path.

Bad People Don't Always Get Theirs

This was always proof to me that God is not real. If God is real, then why are there people that treat others terribly and get away with it? Well, just because someone is bad does not mean they do not have a brain or do not know how to use it. Furthermore, I have seen many people who are "bad" come to God and end up doing good things in the world. Some bad people die being bad and are happy as can be doing so. However, the question is, were they happy? The world will never know.

Remember also that God does not control us; he allows us to be and do as we please. So of course, from that respect it is quite possible to be bad and do well. Where they go when this life is over, however, is between them and God. Don't forget the freewill you were given.

Meeting Believers with No Compassion or Empathy that are Greedy and Abusive

This was also a big argument for me when I was a non-believer. You meet these so-called Christians that have no compassion or empathy whatsoever. They tend to have no problem telling you where you are going to go if you don't adhere to God's word. They put themselves on such a high pedestal that they cannot comprehend the true message of God's word. I have met several Christians like this and it is tough to understand how they believe the way they treat people is Godly. What they are really doing is trying to be the judge, the jury, and the executioner.

Then of course, you have those who are greedy and the abusive. The greedy try to take every last penny you have with a big smile on their face. Money is important in the argument against Christians. Many non-believers, myself included, accuse Christians of being greedy because they ask you consistently to give to the church. This always made me sick. What does money have to do with God?

At my church, they ask us to give and since I own a business, I understand why. Let me explain. Church is separated from state. They still have to pay their utilities, their mortgage, building upkeep, etc. God does not have a wallet nor rain down bucks on churches. I know exactly what it takes to maintain buildings because of the nature of the businesses I own.

It is absolutely a necessity to collect funds from the churchgoers. Furthermore, many church budgets are in the red because people do not generally give enough. I struggled for a few months with Tithing. The concept of it. I mean really, what does God need money for? Well, he doesn't!

Think about this. In Malachi, God is upset that he is being robbed. In Malachi 3:8-11, [8] **"Will a mere mortal rob God? Yet you rob me. But you ask, 'How are we robbing you?' In tithes and offerings. [9] You are under a curse—your whole nation—because you are robbing me. [10] Bring the whole tithe into the storehouse, that there may be food in my house.**

Test me in this, says the Lord Almighty, and see if I will not throw open the floodgates of heaven and pour out so much blessing that there will not be room enough to store it. ¹¹ I will prevent pests from devouring your crops, and the vines in your fields will not drop their fruit before it is ripe, says the Lord Almighty."

Notice that God says, **"Test me in this."** This is the only place in The Bible that I have seen God say to test him, other than this, he is clearly not to be tested. Now let's go to 1 Timothy 6:6-10, **⁶ "But godliness with contentment is great gain. ⁷ For we brought nothing into the world, and we can take nothing out of it. ⁸ But if we have food and clothing, we will be content with that. ⁹ Those who want to get rich fall into temptation and a trap and into many foolish and harmful desires that plunge people into ruin and destruction. ¹⁰ For the love of money is a root of all kinds of evil. Some people, eager for money, have wandered from the faith and pierced themselves with many griefs."**

Notice verse 10. **For the <u>love</u> of money is <u>a</u> root of all <u>kinds</u> of evil.** Do you get it? God wants us to give to make sure that we are putting him first. It is not that he needs our money, but there are others that do. Helping others with your money is a great way to show God that you are putting your love for him first. So, tithing is a necessity. Some in the church clearly abuse the donations given but we must remember that it is not God's fault; it is the churches' fault when it does happen.

Then you have your abusers; these are the worst type. Preying on children or the weak for selfish pleasures that ruin that person's life. There is no excuse. These people are sick. They use God as a tool to prey on their victims to draw them near and twist the word of God to benefit their own perversions. Please, please remember, that this is *not* God's fault. It is those who have chosen to twist his word for their own corruption.

Seeing Families Torn Apart

Families are torn apart for a few main reasons. Financial issues, infidelity, selfishness. However, it is not God who tears the family apart. God wants us to be families and he wants us to live well. You only need to read the word to see that. People will use all sorts of reasons to leave their spouse. Many of the reasons being selfish. God does not break up the family, the people in it do by the *choices* they make.

The worst is when a child dies, and the parents cannot see each other without seeing the child. While I can say I understand how they feel, they still made a lifelong commitment to each other, and they should honor that commitment. Although the circumstances of all these situations are understandable to some degree, it is still a *choice* that *people* make, not God.

Lack of Evidence

People need proof, plain and simple. I understand completely why people need proof, but if God were to show you proof, then faith would be nothing. I was fortunate when I had my experience with The Lord. That was proof enough for me. Although lots of events happened prior to when I felt The Holy Spirit, my proof was that feeling of God's love. This is because my heart was *open* to *allow* God in and *allowed* Him to love me. Solid evidence is something you will never get. The evidence is your love for God and His love for you. When you open your heart to God and His word, you will see and feel the proof.

The bad part about my experience is that I am left with a guilt knowing that not many other people get to have that experience.

Forcing Faith Upon Non-believers and Oppressing Current Believers

Forcing this faith upon non-believers is probably one of the biggest turn offs in the world. People *hate* being told what they are supposed to feel, think, and do. There is nothing worse than when Christians tell you, "You need Jesus, You need to repent or You need to live by God's word." The toughest part about this is that they are right; however, we cannot tell people what to do when it comes across as judgmental or belittling.

As Christians who have been charged with spreading the Word of God, it is extremely frustrating to hear that you cannot minister the word to people who do not want to listen. It is a difficult life. Meanwhile, your heart is aching for people who do not know or fully understand The Word of God.

Now, from the hearer's point of view, how obnoxious is it to sit and listen to some Bible thumpers preach a bunch of nonsense that means nothing?

Wouldn't you think *these people have some real nerve telling me how to live my life and tell me that I should follow this fairytale life that only a delusional person would buy into?*

As the hearer, it is important to bear in mind the courage it takes to minister to a non-believer or even a believer who is not clear on the word and how it really works. You see, it is considered a duty to minister. Christians are not just telling you about The Bible or their beliefs, in their eyes, they are trying to save your spirit by God's command. So many people get irritated when others try to save them. They cannot comprehend why anyone would try to. Most Christians are met with strong backlash by those who do not believe or want to expand their faith. I was one of the people who always dismissed Christians and had even gotten combative with them because I did not want my space or my time invaded. The truth is, I just did not want to hear that I was wrong about anything.

Again, it takes a lot of courage to minister to people knowing that there is a high chance of rejection. So, to the believers, if you do not come on strong and are not judgmental, non-believers might be somewhat more open to your ministering. To the non-believers try taking into consideration that the person ministering to you was commanded by God to do so, even though you don't want to hear it. Try to be polite in your dismissal or, even better, listen to what they say with a little grace and think on it. Even if you dismiss it, at least you gave a person trying to spread God's love a chance.

Peter 3:15-17 — **¹⁵ But in your hearts revere Christ as Lord. Always be prepared to give an answer to everyone who asks you to give the reason for the hope that you have. But do this with gentleness and respect, ¹⁶ keeping a clear conscience, so that those who speak maliciously against your good behavior in Christ may be ashamed of their slander. ¹⁷ For it is better, if it is God's will, to suffer for doing good than for doing evil.**

That is what The Word says. That is one of the things that Christians are trying to follow.

Inability to Have Children When God Tells us to Have Children

I have heard this argument a few times in my life. God does indeed tell us to populate the earth but he does not say you are guaranteed to have a child. Genesis 1:28 says, **²⁸God blessed them and said to them, "Be fruitful and increase in number; fill the earth and subdue it. Rule over the fish in the sea and the birds in the sky and over every living creature that moves on the ground."** There are so many reasons why some people, men and women, can't have children. Children are a blessing, but it is not God that ruins your sperm count or your ovaries so that you cannot have children.

There are circumstances in life that create these situations and many people blame God when those circumstances fall on themselves. Some circumstances are created by none other than ourselves. There are several reasons why we cannot have children. For men, low sperm count can be caused by drugs, depression, physical damage, etc. While for women, abortions, drugs, depression, physical damage, etc., can all be causes for this infertility.

There are of course situations where doctors cannot diagnose the reason why a couple can't have children. Once again, science does not know everything and is not perfect. Not to say that we cannot utilize science in our lives, but we clearly cannot say that science is everything. Just remember that God does not keep you from having a child. It could be environmental, hereditary, or even your fault. If God does not allow you to have a child, maybe it's because you wouldn't make a good parent, maybe you would be a great parent, but the kid would be a demon or maybe it is just not what He wants you to do. Our lives are not ours.

Faith Can Cause Death – Columbine for Example
Millions upon millions have been killed or murdered in the name of God. To "*good*" people who see this happen, it is grounds to ban or discredit God. I cannot say I blame them for the way they feel but they are wrong. That is exactly what we are not supposed to do. We must remain faithful to God as God will hold us accountable for turning our backs to him.

Jesus tells us in The Bible that being faithful to God will result in ridicule, persecution, or even death. It is our duty to stand in faith for God. I am reminded of an awful day, April 20, 1998. Dylan Klebold and Eric Harris ripped through Columbine High School murdering fellow classmates and teachers. I remember that day vividly; I was working for a landscape company, and we were out aerating. I can remember a particular silence over the town I lived in.

Valeen Schnurr was shot by Dylan Klebold. She was laying on the ground bleeding and she prayed to God to not let her die. Dylan turned around and asked her "God? Do you believe in God?" Valeen said, "Yes, I believe in God." Dylan asked her why and she told him "Because it's how my parents raised me." (quoted from Trevin Wax of The Gospel Coalition). Although Dylan did not shoot her again after her confession, she stood for what she believed in even though she had just been shot.

Think about this, she had not only witnessed these guys shooting her classmates, but they also shot her for no reason! And while lying there bleeding to death, she prayed and remained true to her faith. Had Valeen answered no and turned her back to God to save herself, what do you think God would have said? We are warned in The Bible that these things will happen to us. And from what I have read in scripture, we should not rebuke God. So, rebuking God for the benefit of saving our own life is committing the one sin that cannot be forgiven. We should all be so brave as to confess our faith to God in situations that can harm us, like Valeen Schnurr did. A true hero.

This goes back to the subject of ministering to non-believers. They will put themselves in harms way at times to minister the truth knowing that they may be persecuted, ridiculed, fired, demoted, beaten, or killed. What does that say about these people? They are making sacrifices for people who often hate them. So, does God hurt these people? Does God get them killed? No! People make decisions on their own to act the way they do. Remember, we have free will. If a Christian decides not to minister or stand up for his or her faith because of threatening behavior, then God is not first in their life.

It is not to say that Christians should go out and deliberately get themselves killed. It just means that they should not renounce their faith or deny God because they are in danger. Non-believers should see this as devotion and love, not annoying.

People Ditch You: Shunned for Having Faith
I have known people in my life that became Christian or *religious* that I had ejected from my life because of this decision. As a new Christian, I have had some friends not necessarily reject me but keep their distance. Funny thing is, I now try to minister to them whenever I get the chance though I am careful about it.

As a Christian, my job is to spread the word to the world. I do not believe that forcing it on people is the right way to do it. People are fragile these days and unaccepting, especially when it comes to The Word of God. The way we minister is extremely important and cannot be overlooked no matter how wrong the person you are talking to may seem to be. There is a guy on Youtube named Ray Comfort who does a phenomenal job ministering to strangers on the street. The man has grace, and he uses it so well that sometimes it gets me teary eyed.

Your co-workers, friends, even family, may ditch or shun you for being a Christian and you must be prepared for it. It might even hurt, badly. However, you cannot let it deter you from spreading the word or being committed to God. I took special note of the people in my life who thought it was weird that I suddenly stopped cursing.

I stopped cursing because of Dr. Maceo. I noticed that he never used foul language which was admirable to me. Most Christians that I know curse, which in my eyes, makes them somewhat hypocritical. Once I began my walk with God, after a few months, I began to feel like a hypocrite when I cursed so I made it a point to stop. I put a rubber band on my wrist and every time a curse came out, I snapped myself. It was amazing to me that after a noticeably short while, hearing people curse started to hurt my ears, I felt it in my heart.

Now that might sound ridiculous. It is just cursing right? I do not think so. We are told not to curse for a reason. For this, I have had friends that did not necessarily cut me off but backed away some. I became the boring old Christian; a Bible freak. None of them have told me that but I can feel their slight displeasure with my newfound journey. I know I am not as *fun* as I once was.

Why Should We Live in Fear of God?
The Bible says it everywhere; to fear God. I struggle with this myself. If God is love, why do we need to fear him? This concept tends to turn many people away from God because it sounds hypocritical; love this God but fear him. Or else what, is what I

always asked. Well, we know what, we'll get sent to hell or not be able to enter The Kingdom. I always thought that sounded super snotty, stuck up, and just plain wrong, but the cold hard truth is that God gives us specific instructions to not be sent to hell.

The concept of fearing God comes in when you live your life wrong. Fear God because he holds your life in his hands which is why we should be fearful when we disobey God and let it lead us to make the right decisions and amend with God so we can avoid that hot one-way ticket to hell. God does love us and if you have ever felt God's love, you know that there is nothing to fear if you live your life the way He wants you to.

For a long time, I did not really see why it mattered if we were fearful or not. Like I did not really understand why we have to "Love thy neighbor". It all has been made incredibly clear to me now. Think about this, if you were going to offer a large amount of people paradise, wouldn't you want them all to get along? Would you really want to listen to bickering all the time? This is eternity we are talking about here.

It would be taxing to say the least, just like it is here on earth. When we go to heaven, God wants us to get along and I think we have to prove ourselves *before* we go. So that fear should keep us motivated to behave and put God first.

Homosexuality

From the beginning of records, homosexuality has been present. Many argue that Jesus says to love everyone as themselves. This is true of course. However, does loving your neighbor mean breaking God's commandments? I think not. The Bible is clear about sexual immorality. It is intriguing when people make the argument that the term "Homosexuality" did not exist thousands of years ago because what they fail to see is that there were terms used in those times. For example, "man laying with man is an abomination". The original wording in the scrolls was in Greek and was the Greek equivalent of homosexual. So regardless of the terms that were used, it is irrelevant as those scriptures are as plain as day.

Anyone who translates those scriptures any other way is clearly unable to see God's word for exactly what it says. It saddens me to see people fool themselves in this line of thinking. Many LGBTQ+ say they are "born this way". Perhaps that is true but does that mean that it is OK? I am going to part with a nasty secret, this is tough to write in a book that I want to put into the hands of millions. As far back as I can remember, I've always wanted to kill someone. No, I have not killed anyone, and I do not plan on it. However, I have felt these violent tendencies and have felt like I was born this way. In fact, in 2005 I tried to join the Marines so that I could go and kill for my country. I was rejected because of my criminal record. But that doesn't mean that I should go out and kill the guy that cut me off in traffic does it?

So, you see how we are born does not matter. We are given guidelines that are spelled out clearly and we can choose to ignore them and *serve ourselves* instead of God. So, if I am born a sinner, which we are all born in sin, does that mean go out and do as you please? NO! God never said that as long as you are happy with who you are that everything will be OK.

This is really a tough subject for me because my daughter is gay. I love her with all my heart and, even though I will always be there for her and will always love her, I can never *agree* with her. She is one of the sweetest, most genuine, kind, and friendly people I have ever encountered. So, even though I do not *agree* with her, that does not mean I do not *love* her. She makes her own choice and God gave her the freedom to do so. Her judgement is not my place; that is between her and God.

As a Christian who believes that it is our job to spread The Word of God, it is extremely difficult to know the truth and watch the people you love and care about make choices that you know God will not approve of. However, that does not mean that I will abandon those people. It does not mean that I will shun those people. It does not mean that I will judge those people. God told me to love everyone and that is what I will do. I will show them that I love them and that I am here for them no matter what. Of course, my hope is that they will come to God and His Word at some point but again, that is between them and God.

In August 2022, I went to see the head priest at my parnts' Episcopal church to hopefully get answers on why being gay isn't an issue with God. I sought the information at this church because they support LGBTQ+ marriage. Shortly before this, my daughter told me that she was getting married to her girlfriend.

When I went to see the head priest, I was truly hoping that I would find biblical answers through him and learn that I was wrong. We sat down and I voiced my concern to him, I told him that I was concerned that since my daughter was gay that she may not inherit The Kingdom. He told me that a lot of what is written in The Bible is 2000 years old or more and that things have changed.

He went on to say that the story of Sodom and Gomorrah were really about how men would humiliate other men by having sex with them and that it was no so much because of homosexuality as these men did these things, not out of love. So I proceeded to ask him what about Leviticus, how it says that man shall not lay with a man as he does with a woman and that it is an abomination. Abomination is a pretty strong word. He replied that Jesus came to fulfill the law negating that reference.

Wow! So does that mean I can do whatever I want as long as it is in the name love and Jesus? If I kill my wife because she looks at another man and that is how much I love her, does that mean I am good to go? Touchy subject here isn't it. I was becoming very disheartened because I was sitting here with a head priest of a congregation who was responsible for delivering God's Word to hundreds, maybe thousands of people and was writing his own bible right in front of me. He was twisting it for his own gain, for acceptance.

I asked him a question. I asked him what he thought about the fact that Jesus says not to commit sexual immorality (among many other things) or you will not inherit The Kingdom, sexual immorality is clearly defined throughout The bible. His response was that Jesus said that the two most important commandments were to put God first and love thy neighbor as you love yourself. In his eyes, this supersedes that Jesus said to not commit these other sins, especially in a loving homosexual relationship.

I asked him then, since Jesus says that the gate to The Kingdom is Narrow and the road to destruction is wide, would it not make sense that we should be very careful in how we dismiss God's word? I went on and asked him he was sure that he wanted to take that risk being in charge of leading hundreds maybe thousands of people to their possible spiritual death. He gave me a blank look. I went further and told him that my worry was that if what I read in The Bible is true, then how would someone in a gay marriage be able to inherit The Kingdom?

As sinners, Jesus is our path to salvation, if we repent. Repent is key here. How can you repent for something you don't feel bad for? So when you are in a gay marriage, and you go to bed every night and ask for forgiveness it is granted, if you repent. Repent means to turn away from. I am afraid that my daughter and others, will die in their sin meaning, since they do not repent, they will not enter The Kingdom.

When I presented this argument, all he could say was that these were very good questions. I told him that I hope he is right but I don't read the scriptures the way he is manipulating it. Needless to say, I walked out of there feeling very sad and troubled.

While I am no expert in homosexuality. As a new Christian, I believe whole heartedly that we should be true to The Word of God in our churches, in our homes, and in our personal lives. However, we should love those around us and show them that our tolerance is out of love and not out of **worldly pleasures**. Even though The Bible tells us in some instances to stay away from sinners that refuse to rebuke sin, we are still told to love everyone. Here is one of those contradictions. How do you do both? Easy, you just *love* them. You do not have to *agree* with them to *love* them. Show them that you are not a hate monger.

Church

I have heard many times that people do not go to church because they know someone who does. This is one of the saddest statements I have ever heard, mostly because it is true. While I did used to feel that way, it comes back to ministry and how we present ourselves to all people, believers and non.

If we conduct ourselves hypocritically, and then preach to people on how they should live their lives, then it is no wonder that people will not go to church. The worst is when you go to a church and realize that you are not accepted for what you look like. Now, I believe that we should not look inappropriate in the first place, however, if someone walks into your church who appears inappropriate to you, welcome them with open arms, get them involved, learn about *who* they are, work your way into their hearts, love them and expose them to The Word.

Do we even know why we go to church in the first place? It is for fellowship; it is to support one another. Why do we need support? Well, we are on the same team, Team God. When I played lacrosse and was terrible at it, no one really held back on telling me so. It hurt at the time, but I now realize that it was good for me: it made me want more, it made me try harder, it made me serious. When I realized I did not know what it meant to be on a team at lacrosse camp, I knew that I had to do better. When I took being on the team seriously, I improved very fast. That is what church is for. That is why we go. That is why we are supposed to love everyone and why we are supposed to treat each other as we would ourselves. It is because we are on the same team. We just choose not to see it that way. Even more so, we need to show God that we are on His team.

If they are serious about God or are *led* to take God seriously, they will come around on their own as they read The Word and accept it. Let them make the decision, do NOT try to make the decision for them, they will walk out that door and never come back. You do *not* want that. You will become the reason why they hate Christians. *The reason why I used to hate Christians.*

CHAPTER 11

LET US TALK ACCOUNTABILITY

If you are a Christian, you know that it is your job to bring people to God and show grace. However, you may be doing God a huge disservice by judging people that aren't like you even if it is internal judgment (you keep it to yourself, but you still think it). Remember, not even your thoughts are safe from the judgement of God. This line of thinking truly takes on a commitment of changing the way we think, especially if we are unaccepting of those who are different than us. Dr. Maceo once told me about a famous quote by Harold Herring, "The way people think, determines how they will live."

As a business owner, I realize how important accountability is. In fact, I have a theory that to truly be accountable, I have to trace every single problem I have back to myself. Some people I have told this to think I am crazy because not every single problem that is encountered is within my control. Ultimately, I am the one that has to pay for it at the end of the day so it is in my control how I react to it.

Example. I had a guy once attack his crew leader on a job site. He punched him in the face a few times and the crew leader called me and told me what happened. Now, did I punch the employee in the face? No, I did not. Was it my fault? Yes, it was. Why? Because I signed up for the job of liability to my employees and I knew this guy had an attitude. I did not know he was violent but perhaps I should have seen it coming.

The incident brought me to be more careful in who I hire. It also brought me to teach my leaders more humility because the fight started because the crew leader was being arrogant and treating the crew member as if he were less than. I learned a big lesson and since the crew leader was not badly hurt, I was very lucky. Had he been severely hurt, I would have been open to a lawsuit for putting him in harm's way even though I had no idea that something like this would happen.

So now I live my life by asking the question, how is this my fault? I ask this question no matter how much it may not technically be my fault. What matters is that I retrace my steps to see where I went wrong and then make *a change*. The way I think is that I am accountable for everything. The way I live is that I hold myself accountable and have integrity.

Accountability is a way of life. When I read through The Bible, I see accountability everywhere. It is imperative that we learn accountability so that we can identify our faults and make necessary corrections whenever we need to. If you cannot hold yourself accountable for anything, make no mistake about it, you *will* be held accountable.

Believers and non-believers alike, are more interested in their wants over their needs. Of course, we are raised in a society that teaches us this. This is because we are taught that everything that is morally wrong is common so it is not that bad. Normalizing these things is what is killing us. The lack of accountability in our lives grooms us to exponentially accelerate our own demise.

CHAPTER 12

Conclusion

Not everyone can understand the law, The Word, the severity of how important it is to follow it. Remember Rob? As much as I hate to admit it, everything Rob said was true. You cannot walk around doing whatever you want and then at the zero hour say, "I love Jesus"! and be saved. It is a shame what he decided to do with his life and throw it all away, he could have been a great minister. Instead, he not only ruined his life but Marissa's as well.

Although I did not know Marissa on any intimate or close level, I did run into her at a surprising place about ten years after Rob pursued a relationship with her. I went out one night to a Gentleman's club with a few friends. At some point a dancer approached me and asked me into the V.I.P. lounge. There the dancer performed and as we talked I was shocked to see who it was. It was Marissa!

I could not believe it. I can honestly say that I was humiliated for myself and for her. At that moment, I realized that I never wanted to go into one of these places again and I was not even a Christian then. I also realized what a tragedy it can be as to how people are influenced in their youth. Would

Marissa have ended up this way if not for Rob? Who knows? What brought *me* there? Was I so much better? I think not.

How many people could be great ministers of The Word? How many people have great charisma and use it solely to make money, run companies, or get their own way? A lot I imagine. Those are the people that can use God's Word for good and spread the word like wildfire. They could be a good influence to lead people *to* God—instead, they lead them *away* from God.

The worst thing we can do as Christians is be doom and gloom ministers. We should be helping God shed his light on people who are in need, not casting down darkness and misery. One of the main takeaways I got from reading The New Testament was that Jesus very much wants us to spread The Word. In fact, he charges us with spreading God's Word.

Although I did not get to know him long term, G.W. (remember him?) was a genuine soul. He did not have the greatest sense of humor, but he did take his faith seriously, and that was when he was seventeen. I ran into G.W. about three or four years ago (I was around forty) at the movie theater and he was with his wife who was his girlfriend back in high school. While I am sure they have had their fair share of problems, I remember thinking how impressive it was that they were still together.

At the time of running into G.W. at the movie theater, it was awkward. This was because I had nothing in common with him anymore. In fact, I did not have anything in common with him back then either, other than the enjoyment of drawing comic books. Since G.W. was a faithful Christian, he always had an aura of perfection over others. An attitude that made him come off as better than everybody else. Well, you know what? He was better than everybody else.

I think our class had about 300 to 400 people in it and our school had 1200 or so total students. Out of all of those students, he was the only one that stood out and made you think he was full in spirit. He was not arrogant, rude, or judgmental.

He never started trouble. He was kind, quiet, and faithful to his belief. Most of all, he was sincere. He was always better than the rest of us. G.W. carried God's light down the halls of the school and shined it in darkness. We should all be so brave.

As I was writing this section of this book, G.W.'s real name escaped me. In fact, I'm not sure I ever knew it. I dug out my old comic book drawings in search of the only drawing he made and signed that I had a copy of. I finally found it and, on another sheet that was next to the drawing, I found three Bible verses that were written in my handwriting. They were, **1 Corinthians 11:12-16** regarding long hair on men, **Matthew 5:38-48** regarding fighting and **Matthew 22:34-40** regarding attitude. It was kind of strange thinking about it because I have had those drawings (at least 300) out and shuffled around them many times and those two were still right next to each other. I wrote the verses down because G.W. was trying to witness to me. He had been telling me that I was living my life wrong. He tried to guide me on my long hair, my serious attitude problem, and my joy of fighting. What a guy! Seventeen years old and trying to save a fellow student while trying to make a real friend. I wish I could run into G.W. today, I would have so much to say to him. If you're out there old friend, I am sorry.

I made so many mistakes in my life. For decades I walked around thinking about how backwards it was when that judge said to me that he would have done exactly what I did but the law is the law. What hypocrisy! But why didn't it sit right with me? Why was I still angry about it and let it linger in my thoughts all of those years? Well, it was because I was wrong.

I did not *defend* my brother's honor, I *avenged* it. My brother was not in danger. He was not injured. I was. I was still harboring the injury from my failure when we were kids growing up when I antagonized the biggest bully in my school for no reason. I brought the entire situation on myself because of my own stupidity and even though I did not make Shelby threaten my brother, my reaction was my fault.

This is why I find it important to always trace my problems back to myself by analyzing the situation and dissecting it further until *I* am the only factor left, even if I wasn't the direct cause of the problem in question. This is how I hold myself accountable for my actions. It helps me see what I could have done better, differently. This is important because it leads me to a better path in life. If only others would do the same, this world would be a much better place to live.

When I look back to my parents, they inadvertently taught me this lesson by holding me accountable and laying tough love on me. When I talk to my parents about the affairs my mom had they both completely admit that they were both at fault. At first, I did not understand this mentality because my mom cheated. How could my dad be responsible? Well, it takes two.

After all, Marriage is a place where you respect, love, and fulfill each other's needs. My dad did not do that. My parents fought constantly when I was a kid. I have heard many people say that kids are better off having their parents separate to avoid bringing them up in a turbulent environment. No! If anything, kids might learn how to problem solve, or learn how they *do not* want to be when they grow up. Of course, there are situations where parents should not even have access to their children like in cases of abuse.

I always said that I would only get married once. I meant it. Strange that I had that mentality even though I never believed in God and my parents never instilled that in me. I watched them come to the brink of destruction more than once and the main lesson I took away from it was that when you are married, you are committed, and you have a duty to one another. Yes, it was awful listening to them fight constantly. Yes, I thought about running away during those times. Yes, there were times I wanted different parents. However, let me tell you this. I cannot think of two people who could have been better parents to me.

I learned commitment, perseverance, and accountability. Not just to my wife, my kids, and myself, but to God as well. I cannot think of a better lesson to learn from two better people. My parents did not just teach me commitment to the above, they also taught me commitment to my job and how important it is to perform well, along with being respectful to my boss. They taught me that if I want to have a good life, I must work hard for it.

One of the problems we have in life today is that people have forgotten how to work hard for what they want, or even need. In fact, all people do is want. It appears many people can't be happy without all of the *things* that they *want*. People will go into massive amounts of debt and ruin their lives for the sake of having *expensive possessions*. I wish I could say that I have not behaved this way myself. I wish even more that I could say that I am not *still* paying for it.

The one *thing* that most of the people who *lust* for *material possessions* cannot say, is that they have God. We work for *material possessions* when God tells us to work for *him*. **"Commit everything you do to The Lord, and He will establish your plans"—Proverbs 16:3**. This means, he will establish the plans *He* wants *you* to follow. God wants us to live a fruitful life; He wants us to be comfortable. The problem is, we do not know it because we are not willing to read His word, and so many of us are left to our own defenses when we really should be asking Him for His input and guidance. We should be following his word and abiding by it. If *what you desire* never comes, did He abandon you? Let's look at *you*. Did *you* feel his love? Were *you* listening? Were *you* feeling Him? Did *you* care about *His* needs? Did *you* obey? **Psalms 37:4 says: "Take delight in The Lord and HE will give you the desires of your heart."** This means, as you glorify God and enjoy Him, He will mold your heart to give the desires that HE wants you to have.

Have you ever noticed that people who have all their desires when their life starts to unravel, they sometimes blame God, or claim that God isn't real because their lives are miserable? We *all* know someone like that. Is it God's fault? When babies die, when innocent people die, when people get cancer, when good workers lose their jobs and end up homeless...is it God's fault? No, it is not God's fault. Remember this, God gave us the freewill to make our own decisions in life and go down the paths that we so choose. God has a plan for all of us, but, it is up to *us* to learn how to hear his voice and how to follow *His* plan for us. Things that happen to us that are out of our control, however, are simply things that are out our control, environmental, situational, etc.

Proverbs 19:3; A person's own folly leads to their ruin, yet their heart rages against the Lord. This is tough to see when you do not understand.

Let's just say that your misery was God's doing, let's say that he valued you enough to punish you on earth for not doing his will, whose fault would that be? You were given free will to follow Him and obey yet you were so full of pride and arrogance that you decided that you didn't need God if he was just going to hurt you. Well, did you hurt him?

There are so many questions that we have about God. We could likely all go on for days and get nowhere because there are just some questions that only God can answer. Aliens, the beginning of time, evolution, death, life, the world, are all questions that we ask, as believers and non-believers alike. On Christmas 2021, my family and I were sitting around the fire talking about these questions. My dad was asking some of them because I had been giving him consistent explanations for his questions based on my reading in The Bible. As strange as it may sound, he asked me the questions above that The Bible does not necessarily tackle and an answer came to me that I was not prepared for. It just rolled out: "Dad, all I can say is that there are definitely questions that I can't answer but I do know this, I have felt The Holy Spirit and once you have felt The Holy Spirit, it doesn't really matter."

Throughout my entire life, I thought that these crazy Christian people were hypocrites, selfish, lame...and the problem. However, after feeling The Holy Spirit in me, after feeling God's love and *knowing* that He is real, I realize, the problem...was actually me.